Environment Preservation
A Philosophical Critique

Environment Preservation

A Philosophical Critique

by

Sashinungla

Decent Books
New Delhi

Cataloging in Publication Data — DK
[Courtesy: D.K. Agencies (P) Ltd. <docinfo@dkagencies.com>]

Sashinungla, 1975-
Environment preservation: a philosophical critique / by Sashinungla.
viii, 152 p. 23 cm.
Includes bibliographical references (p.)
Includes index.
ISBN 8186921311

1. Environmental protection – Philosophy.
2. Philosophy of nature. 1. Title.

DDC 363.700 1 21

ISBN 81-86921-31-1
First Published in India in 2005

Published and printed by:
Decent Books
D-36/A-1, Mohan Garden
Najafgarh Road
New Delhi - 110 059
Ph. (011) 2535-3435

Distributed by:
D.K. Printworld (P) Ltd.
Regd. office : *'Sri Kunj,'* F-52, Bali Nagar
New Delhi - 110 015
Phones : (011) 2545-3975, 2546-6019; *Fax* : (011) 2546-5926
E-mail : dkprintworld@vsnl.net
Web : www.dkprintworld.com

Preface

BUILDING the broken linkages between ecology, economics and ethics has become significant. It is with this spirit that the environmental preservation ethics is taking its core from the tribal ecological wisdom. The present book is based on my Ph.D thesis submitted to the NEHU, Shillong in July 2002. Without the outstanding support of my supervisor, the much-admired Prof. Sujata Miri, this work would not have been completed. She first got me interested in the study of environmental philosophy, especially from a traditional tribal perspective when I was a post-graduate student. Since then she has provided invaluable encouragement, advice, and, when needed, criticism of the theoretical arguments I make. Were it not for our conversations together, the key concepts in which I work out the argument between environmental crisis, modern preservation schemes and tribal eco-worldview would be one 'insight' short. I am grateful to her for her continuing mentorship. I also would like to thank Decent Books for its patience in waiting for the final manuscript and for encouraging me throughout the process of getting this book published.

Finally, I extend my deepest gratitude to the unwavering support of a network of friends — Pankaj, Siby, Zoher, Arpita, Naffissa, Shubadi, Mridulda and Bibo and my family who have cheerfully endured the trials of research work and the stresses of writing a book. Thanks to mum and dad for their interest in my work and steady encouragement over the years, and to my friend Vikas for never giving up faith in me and my work. I feel pleased that I have friends who are keen about my academic quests.

Contents

For Mum & Dad,
with love and thanks for giving me encouragement
and space to do what I needed to do.

1

Introduction

THE present-day world is seen as one in which scientific knowledge is faltering, a world in which the concept of environment and its preservation are in urgent need of redefinition because they pose a problem not only for the philosophers but have threatened the very survival of our earth. Hence, it is inevitable to first situate the man-nature problem on the map of philosophical discourse for the sake of highlighting the relevance of the critique undertaken here.

In the West, the philosophy of nature and the philosophy of man have developed along different, and sometimes antithetical routes, which has been at the root of our mistaken notion that nature is "there' to be harnessed, subdued and exploited. This empirically oriented positivist philosophy in the West, provides the philosophical justification for the ruthless, exploitative, mechanistic paradigm, which has caused so much damage to our environment.

With the advancement of science a new idea of the human relationship with nature emerged. In such a world-view, ethics and cosmology are completely separate from, and have nothing to do, with each other (particularly stressed by various schools of positivist philosophy). This modern mindset, in its understanding of the world and of nature, of reality, of history, and of self, has peeled away the assumptions of man and nature's inter-relatedness. Humans are able to understand, predict, and control everything relating to the world, to the extent of thinking that humans are now separate from, and masters of, the earth. The modern mind has constructed "a view of reality, nature and life with unqualified justification." Here, natural resources are given value only in so far as they are useful for the development of science and technology.

In sharp contrast with this is the pre-modern world-view, where the ethics of a people and their view of the physical universe co-define each other. In those world-views, which survived the test of time and were found sustaining by the people that adopted them, there is coherence between the value system or ethical code of the people and their other beliefs, so that the universe appears to be a harmonious place, supportive of human existence. That coherence is gone from the scientific world-view. And, I tend to think, if the modern man finds the universe a hostile lonely place it is our world-view that has made it so for us.

What is nature? What is man's place in nature? What should human relationship with nature be? And how is Environmental Preservation possible? The discussion and answer to these questions constitute the core of the critique undertaken here.

In the second chapter, I try to clarify the meaning of some basic concepts such as, Environment, Nature and Preservation. The dictionary meaning of environment as stated is "the region, surroundings or circumstances in which anything exists; everything external to the organism." [1] Thus, the environment of the human being is seen to include the abiotic factors of land, water, atmosphere, planet, sounds, odours and tastes; the biotic factors of animals, plants, bacteria and viruses; and the cultural factors of economic, social and political.

Again, nature can be understood as the totality of things. Nature is like a living and growing organism suffused with life and intelligence. Some regard nature as a pure machine, directed by divine intelligence. Others say nature is neither permeated by mind nor is it a mechanism in the hand of its mechanic, but it is a self-transforming system, essentially temporal whose development is best understood through the analogies of biological evolution or human history.

I have posed the question as to whether man is part and parcel of nature or not. To consider man as part and parcel of nature emphasizes the continuity of human, animal, organic and inorganic worlds and suggests that human behaviour may be amenable to the same kind of investigations that are effective in studying other domains of nature. And to set man against nature is to emphasize his distinctiveness such as rationality, creativity and freedom, whereas nature is seen as lacking these attributes.

I have discussed briefly the concept of nature as viewed by different thinkers at different times, from the ancients understanding of nature and earth as "oikas'. (the ancient vision of earth as a single public household) to the modern ecologists' and environmentalists' varied ways of analysing environment to study and compare the different components. Though in most traditions there is a definite emphasis

---

1. *Encyclopedic Dictionary of Environment*, vol. I, eds. G.R. Chhatwal, D.K. Pandey, K.K. Nanda, New Delhi:Anmol Publications, 1988, p. 238.

on the sacredness of the environment, and man's ideas, and attitude towards its own habitat find a crystal clear place in his language and literature, yet the talk of environmental science is a unique contemporary phenomenon.

The first all-important fact, which I have emphasized, is that life apart from environment does not exist, and cannot be conceived. Life consists essentially of a process of interchange between the life-substance-on the environment. The term environment apart from reference to life is, meaningless.

Confronted with the so-called environmental crisis there is much demand today for environmental preservation. Contemporary man has anxiously started thinking for environmental issues, with various dimensions. Gradually, as the effects of rapid and often uncontrolled industrialization have become evident, the emphasis has shifted from the study of nature to a desire to preserve it.

When asked why should we try to preserve our environment? The answer goes far beyond a desire to preserve beauty of unspoiled, or natural areas, although this could be a very important reason. A popular explanation is that man needs to preserve the balance in nature, for if that is destroyed man will have no place else to go. And, this explanation is available to people irrespective of whether they are biologists, or culturalists, aesthetists or educationalists. The problem with this approach — as with modernity as such — is, of course, that it is too human-centered for it to be able to give an adequate meaning to the concept of preservation as applied to non-humans.

The central ethical issue raised in the history of environmental philosophy has been — "what kind of relationship should be between man and nature?" It can be answered either by seeing man as part of nature or by seeing man as apart from nature. This is largely my concern in the third chapter. Here, I have tried to bring out the different approaches regarding man and nature transaction, with the intention to unfold the western anthropocentric concept of nature. Different thinkers throughout the ages have tried to consider the problem of the relationship between man and nature, such as Galileo, J.S. Mill and Bacon on the one hand, and Spinoza on the other.

I found that Western anthropocentric thought places man at the centre of the universe, hence, its understanding of man-nature relationship reflect its central position. As such, it made the doors open for further scientific investigation of nature. There are many implications of the scientific thesis as regards the concept of nature. One of the most important implications is the distinction between man and nature on the basis of rationality. Given the view that man is the only conscious being, environment becomes an object. Therefore, the advice is that environment must be exploited to the fullest for the benefit of man.

So, modern man after the Age of Reason does not have any respect for the environment. He does not realize that by destroying the environment, he destroys himself. This destruction of the environment has led to the environmental problem; I take this environmental problem to be a moral problem. This means that there has been a moral crisis with regard to the understanding of the environment. Therefore, there is a need to rethink about the relationship between man and the environment. Even if we were to recognize the mandate of man over environment in an industrialized world — the real question at the present context is whether environment should be treated as a pure scientific-cum-economic subject or as a scientific-cum-economic-cum ethical issue?

Ethics as defined by moral philosophers is a statement of the most fundamental principles of conduct. It is an attempt to answer the question of what is right and wrong in a systematic way. Encarta Encyclopedia defined environmental ethics as:

> A field of applied ethics concerned with those issues that arise when human beings interact with the natural environment. It not only seeks to evaluate past and present attitudes and practices, but aims to offer guidance as to how people ought to think about, and conduct, their relationship with the natural environment; for example, environmental ethicists debate whether the natural environment is simply an exploitable resource for human interests, or whether it has significance independent of any use that might be made of it, a value that ought to constrain practices.[2]

Holmes Rolston conceived environmental ethic as "one whose fundamental principles are responsive to environmental considerations."[3] Thus environmental ethic is a code of behaviour to protect environment from degradation. I

---

2. *Encarta Encyclopaedia*, 2000, pp. 1993-99.
3. See Holmes Rolston III, "Is there an ecological Ethics?" *Ethics* 85 (1975) : 93-109, reprinted in Rolston, *Philosophy Gone Wild* (Buffalo, New York: Prometheus Books (1986 : 12-29).

have examined in this connection the claim that environmentally ethical conduct is based on ecologically sound principles which lead to environmentally sensible decisions.

Earlier man thought of his ethics in relations to other people, God, or himself. He has thought of it very little in terms of his relations to other animals and still less, if at all, in terms of what he do or how he "relates" to nature. Lately, however (after being aware of the role that the modern scientific attitude played in the degradation of the environment) going beyond a mechanistic fragmented world-view, some trends of contemporary scientific theories have opened up a new world-view of oneness of the universe, which includes not only our natural environment but also our fellow human beings. The question of nature as the ground of human value has become the centre of modern thinker's concern, a kind of locus around which all other considerations have been revalued. And this concern is available from ecology, whether shallow or deep. However, there are differences in their approach.

Ethical views on the man and nature relationship are diverse and many, while it is not within the purview of this work to provide a detailed account of each of them, rather, it is addressed to a more general preliminary issue which is being much discussed in recent ecological literatures. To cite but few, Andrew Brennan's position of ecological humanism, Paul Taylor's biocentric ethic of respect for nature, and Holmes Rolston's determined holistic approach.

In the fourth chapter, I have attempted an analysis of certain specific attempts at environmental preservation, to uncover inconsistencies, if any. With this objective in my mind, I survey, first of all, briefly though, the history of environmental movements. However, the survey is less exhaustive than selective, since I am concerned with only those movements, which will have a direct bearing on environment preservation. Hence, beginning with the people's movements of Chipko and Bishnois, I traverse through the heartfelt call of the modern scientific man for a new form of community-academic partnership, and a revaluing of tribal-eco-world-view. In between I scan modern man's attempts to salvage the environment by ways of different conservation programmes like forestation, and their "sustainable development" *mantra,* highlighting in them, however, only select aspects.

Starting at least as early as the 1960s the practice of clear felling in the name of industrialization and development met with a lot of opposition from the environmentalists, who argued that it was destroying wildlife habitat, reducing diversity of flora and fauna, and causing soil erosion. Thus, when it comes to management of forests, the timber industry and environmentalists have traditionally been and are at loggerheads with it. Whoever wins, the losers are generally people from communities living near the forest. Though with the inception of the idea of a sustainable development, they found that their causes had some common ground, forest health and community stability. Of course, as I have mentioned earlier, recently there is a lot of lip service about the importance of involving the interest of the local people. Even then, the question still remains — has anything changed? Few examples remain an exception. The old story continues at higher levels.

I have argued that modern environmental preservation programme do not basically cater to the actual needs and environments of their citizens; they are only domains of influence and affluence of national and multinational elites and powers. It is so because despite many global attempts the ecological crisis is still on its march. And the remedy has been worse than the problem itself, since the superstructure is made to rest on a vacuum.

I tend to believe that proper attention to today's environmental crisis requires not just to remake the world economy, technology and planning, but also a complete spiritual renewal from within. So, the question is — which world-view will provide the basis to attain this ideal? I believe, quite sensibly, that our current — market and technology driven — world is not a desirable one under this situation, and that a new way of thinking based on the one's traditional values will offer a more evaluative concern for the environment and its preservation.

While discussing at length that the prevailing modern preservation strategy is flawed in itself to provide us with a satisfactory ethics to the present environmental crisis, I have tried to drive home the point as to which ethics is best, towards the preservation of environment. In other words, I have criticized an exclusively anthropocentric approach and have tried to explore a non-anthropocentric environmental ethics in the tribal world-view.

In chapter five, I turn away, therefore, from the entire Western and modern debate and try and see, if there is a way out in traditional tribal thought and practice. In this connection, I have attempted an analysis of the traditional world-view of the Aos regarding objects of nature with the objective of discovering their concept of nature. I have discovered that according to them, there are no distinct categories namely, man and nature. The legends of the Ao relate the continuous dialogue between man and the natural forces. Their relationship is one of give and take and what holds good for nature holds also for man. The Aos respect trees, rivers, rocks and other natural entities as their guardians and teachers, which they say protect the people from evil forces. The plants and animals are the helpers and the friends of Ao people.

For Aos, the concept of religion and the concept of nature co-define each other. They have a fantastically formulated belief about the concept of "salvation," which centres on man's philosophy of life, in relation to his environment. In other words, for the Aos man's salvation cannot be understood apart from the well being of the whole creation. They say:

> *nangnu sungdonglidong sararur mesenmetula hemshibala meytsungba kimako metetjokbeo.*

Which means, if you do not care for the trees and the animals, you'll be dealt with severely on the day of *meyutsungba*.[4]

At this point, it may be asked — how could the traditional tribal society maintain such an eco-world-view? I have discovered that, for the Aos, it was possible through the practice of their *sobaliba*, which embodies the traditional etiquette, social manner, honesty, integrity, virtues and much more than that. Commenting on the concept of Ao *sobaliba*, Renthy Keitzar said "we cannot explain such

---

4. According to the Ao tradition, Meyutsungba is considered as the supreme judge on a person's death, whose judgement is purely based on the man's earthly deeds.

traditional code of morals, but these can be understood." In short, it is this principle that makes the eco-vision of the Aos a reality.

My concluding chapter proceeds in two unequal parts. In the first part, I briefly summarize my results of the critique undertaken. In the second part, I pursue, though rather tentatively, certain corollaries of this study, which, hopefully, will keep me busy for the many more years to come. It is hoped that this may also suggest research themes for the development of the eco-world-view of traditional tribals. These corollaries are tentative because they will have to be worked out in greater detail.

The various discussions of the environment and its preservation that I have carried on to in the previous chapters, I think are ample evidence of the fact that Western thought by and large, has tended to see man along with his culture as opposed to the concept of nature. It can be pointed out that many views about the relationship between man and nature is rooted in the centrality of the man and the subordinate position accorded to the rest of creation. Environment and its preservation are conceived to have value only in relation to the benefit they can confer to human beings.

The work is not intended to analyse any particular philosopher, nor any set of philosophers, but the essence, and above all the consequences, of the whole philosophical mode of an epoch. Most of all, the intention is to investigate what changes must be made in this mode of thought to make philosophy a truly supportive tool in our quest for environmental preservation. Therefore, we need to rethink our relationships with the world at large, by abandoning the mechanistic conception of the world, and by replacing it with a much broader value based one. I subscribe to a tribal eco-world-view.

The modern man as I have pointed out is at his best in exploiting nature. He fails to realize that the growth of all civilization whether traditional or modern depends primarily upon the materials of nature. Interestingly, the ancient tribals understood this fact when they insisted on the close connection between man and nature.

Generally, the concept of nature means the physical and material things of the universe, which is diametrically contrasted, with the concept of culture and that of the subjective aspects. But this is not true in case of the Ao concept of nature and many other tribal people of north-east India. It will be important to ask and seek to answer the question whether or not in the Ao view of things man even with his various special qualities is set against nature as two distinct categories of being. I have discovered that there is no sharp distinction between the world of things and the world of culture among the Aos. In other words, the Ao world of culture is to be explained in terms of the world of nature. The Ao concept of nature by its etymological meaning is a general conception about the universe as a whole. It will include their idea of Man, God and Nature.

It is only recently that Western thought is associating the concept of man with the concept of nature. (Trying to retrieve the tribal eco world-view by the ecologist is one desperate example of this.) The emergence of such a new conception of nature is making man appreciative of his place in the natural order.

2

Concept of Environment Preservation

THE concept of nature is popularly viewed as opposed to the concept of culture. Although, the world of nature is undoubtedly related to the world of culture. If we look for the ways in which people (or individuals) cope with their natural environment, we will almost necessarily, find the physical man with cultural equipment at his disposal for this purpose. Thus, the same physical environment may have quite different meanings for; say a food-gathering Pygmy, an agricultural Bantu or a Western European.

When people assume environment as surroundings, it indicates different meanings. As for a teacher in a classroom it will be his students, blackboard, etc., for a housewife, it will be her house, kitchen, etc. Such kind of a conception regarding environment has been categorized by some scholars in the term microenvironment. This micro-environment designates a functional environment, i.e., specific environment of specific organisms. Literally, this term refers to a small environment. But it has been somewhat a relative term. Therefore, this term is used for the immediate environment of an organism.

Nature is often seen viewed as "culturally constructed." Because different individuals, times, and societies construct particular versions of nature in so far as they interpret it in different ways in and through cultural categories and values. "We cannot experience nature except through the lens of meanings assigned to it by particular cultures and periods." [1] These meanings affect attitudes towards nature. "Nature carries an immensely complex and contradictory symbolic load."[2] "The idea of nature contains, though often unnoticed, an extraordinary amount of human history."[3] Here, Soper and Williams are making the claim that ideas about nature are historically and culturally determined. There is no single essential "nature" that all individuals in all places and times recognize as such or can access outside the mediations of human culture.

Another view is that — nature is seen as literally, physically constructed by human society. According to this view, not only do cultural concepts mediate our experience of it but most of what we refer to as "nature," from city parks to rain forests, has in fact been shaped by human actions. Thus, very little of the world today remains "natural" if that means free of human intervention. Modern industrial cultures, of course, have had many more far-reaching effects on the non-human world. As Soper wrote "In our own time the human impact on the environment has been so extensive that there is an important sense in

1. Anna Peterson, "Environmental Ethics and the Social Construction of Nature," *Environmental Ethics* (winter 1999) : 34.
2. Kate Soper, *What is Nature?*, Oxford: Blackwell, 1995, p. 2.
3. Raymond Williams, "Ideas of Nature," in *Problems in Materialism and Culture* (London: verso, 1980) : 69.

which it is correct to speak of nature as itself a cultural product or construction."[4] According to Bill Mckibben, climate changes caused by the burning of fossil fuels have altered all global ecosystems so extensively that we can no longer speak of a "nature" free from human intervention: "the planet is utterly different now."[5] Perhaps, both versions of social construc-tionism remind us that nature and culture, in their myriad forms, interact with each other, in our minds and also in the physical world.

Against this version of social construction regarding nature, several writers have offered a qualified or "soft" realism. Soper, one of the most articulate advocates of this position, argues that while it is true that any distinction we make between the reality of nature and its cultural representation is itself conceptual, it does not follow that . . . there is no ontological distinction between the ideas we have of nature and what the ideas are about: that nature is only signified in human discourse, inverted commas "nature" is nature, and we should therefore remove the inverted commas.[6]

The concept of environment is seen as differing from age to age. To be totally candid and faithful to the present problem concerning environment, it could be said without hesitation that the present concept and problem of environment are totally different from the olden times. Though in most traditions there is a definite emphasis on the sacred-

---

4. Kate Soper, *What is Nature?*, Oxford: Blackwell, 1995, p. 152.
5. Bill Mckibben, *The End of Nature*, New York: Random House, 1989, p. 49.
6. Kate Soper, *What is Nature?*, Oxford: Blackwell, 1995, p. 47-58.

ness of the environment, and man's ideas and attitude towards its own habitat find a crystal clear place in his language and literature, yet the talk of environmental science is a unique contemporary phenomenon.

The ancients understand nature and earth as oikas (the ancient vision of earth as a single public household). The oikas itself is at home in both classical Greek and "Streek Greek" of the New Testament. The first and basic meaning of oikas is simply "Habitat earth." Habitat is the core meaning of all eco words: economy, ecology, ecumenicity itself.[7] Here, oikas — earth as a vast but single household of life — means the capacity of survival, that is, sustainable habitat. It means space and the means for the living of all living things. Thus, the ancient people understand that without adequate hospitable habitat, nothing lives. Not only humans, but all life-forms used carefully fit habitats.

Likewise, they defined the concept of ecology-logos as — the logic of the house or knowledge of the structures and dynamics of the household, how it has been configured and runs. Ecology here, thus means knowing, from inside, the interested dynamics that make up the total life of the household and the requirements for living together. This is to respect creation's integrity and live in accord with it.

For the ancient people, Oikas as a vision is not the enlightenment project, an earth ethic grounded in the universally human as some core that can be stripped of particularity and exist independently of differences generated by race, gender, class, and culture. There is no

---

7. S.R. Joshi, N. Joshi, *Man and His Environment*, Shillong: Gautam Bros., 1999, pp. 23-24.

core human nature so solid that differences are normatively insignificant. Nor is the Oikas, an earth ethic held together by universal norms and procedures secured through the power of shared universal reason as a capacity that somehow leaves the peculiar treasures and passions of time and place behind. But, earth as Oikas sees these provincialities as the diverse and finite units of a greater community to which they intrinsically belong.

The earlier Vedic thinkers too had developed the concept of "cosmic" nature. They believed that there is a particular order in the universe and nature has its own system of manifestation. The worldly things do not indicate any arbitrary nature. They are bound by certain rules. Thus the nature and natural powers move in a definite periphery and there is regularity in all-natural phenomena. There is something "unchangeable" on the background of the changeable. This unchangeable regularity of nature was termed as *ṛta* by Vedic thinkers.[8]

The primary feature of the medieval attitude towards nature was characterized as an unchanging order, with anything in its place, and since people found their place within that order, they had no impetus to rearrange nature or to study it in order to determine its law. The harmony of human kind with nature was such that there were no such efforts to stand apart from it and analyse it. The universe was experienced more of as a sociologist might observe it and, since the conviction of the order, nationality, and

8. N.B. Marathe, "Environmental Awareness as Reflected in Ancient Sanskrit Literature," in *Proceedings of the National Seminar on Environmental Awareness Reflected in Sanskrit Literature,* Poona: Centre of Advanced Study in Sanskrit, 1991, pp. 231-235.

fundamental changelessness of the universe was so great, there was little interest in observing nature for its own sake, one could as well determine how a body fell by thinking about its fall, as by measuring its fall. Thus, medieval science approach to nature was in nature primarily deductive.

On the other hand, modern ecologists have tried various ways of analysing environment to study and compare their different components, but no single system is completely satisfactory. Biology tells us that the transaction between man and nature is always circular, always a feedback. Human ecology cannot be limited strictly to biological concepts, but it cannot ignore them. It emerges from biological reality and grows from the fact of inter-connection as a general principle of life.

So, for a biologist the problems raised by the term environment are also basically concerned with the role of a particular factor or a group of factors, which play a role in the process of evolutionary change. To what extent can the characters of human beings be changed by changes in the condition under which they live; and, if such changes occur, how far can they become permanent; are some of the rudimentary questions concerning human surroundings. Since there exists a definite relationship between man and his environment, any change in the latter certainly brings about frequent changes in the natural organisms.

In an era of ecological breakdown, answering the questions — what is nature? What is Man's place in nature: And what is the relationship of Man to the natural world? — has become a momentous importance for our everyday lives and for the future that we and other life — forms face. These are serious philosophical questions that should be reflected upon. One should not answer them in an offhand way, with poetic metaphors or unthinking, visceral reactions. The definitions and ethical standards with which we respond to them may ultimately decide whether human society will creatively foster natural evolutions, or whether we will render the planet uninhabitable for all complex life forms, including ourselves.

At first glance, everybody *knows* what nature is. It is that which *humanity* is coating with petroleum or destroying. But such *prima facie* definitions fall apart when we examine them with some care. "If nature is indeed what is all around us, we may reasonably ask, then, is a carefully manicured suburban lawn not alive? Is the split-level house it surrounds, not nature? Are its furnishings not natural?"[9]

Today, this sort of question is likely to elicit a heated avowal that only "wild," "primordial," or even non-human nature is authentically natural. Other people, no less thoughtful, will reply that nature is basically matter or the materialized stuff of the universe in all its forms — what philosophers sweepingly call *Being*. The fact is that wide philosophical differences have existed for centuries in the west over the very definitions of the word *Nature*. These differences remain unresolved to this day, even as nature is making headlines in environmental issues that are of enormous importance for the future of all life forms.

Nature, in its widest sense, can mean the totality of things all that would have appeared in an inventory of the universe. Nature consists of all elements of matter. It also

---

9. Murray Bookchin, *The Philosophy of Social Ecology: Essays on Dialectical Naturalism*, New Delhi: Rawat Publications, 1996, p. 2.

means the hills, mountains, rivers, trees, etc. We may ask the philosophical questions about nature: What is nature (natural) being contrasted with in this context? The straightforward answer will be that nature is contrasted with the artificial or conventional. Nature can be taken as the mere raw materials, for instance, the stone, tree, etc. While the artificial or conventional are seen as the inferences, modifying by an alien causality, the characteristic patterns of behaviour. Natural is unfinished and preparatory, requiring artifice to complete and crown it. Nature is like a living and growing organism as suffused with life and intelligence. Some say that nature is a pure machine, directed by divine intelligence. Another view is that nature is neither permeated by mind nor is it a mechanism in the hand of its mechanic, but it is a self-transforming system, essentially temporal, whose development is best understood through the analogies of biological evolution or human history. Nature is a cluster of everything found in the universe as a whole.

In the case of man, we have to consider the cultural as well as the biological and physical environments. Thus, the sum of the forces and materials in any situation can be looked at as the total environment, but again this is seen as including many elements that have no influence on behaviour. We live, for instance, in the magnetic field of the earth, but this does not affect our physiology in any known way; and we cannot perceive viruses without instruments, but many of them do affect us by causing disease. Viruses would, and then form part of our operational environment, although not a part of our perceptual environment.

Defining nature becomes an even more complex task when we include the human species as part of it. Is human society with the ensemble of technologies and artefacts — not to speak of such ineffable features as its conflicting social interacts and institutions — any less part of nature than non-human beings are part of nature, are they merely one life-form among many others, or are they unique in ways that place major responsibilities on them with respect to the rest of the world of life, responsibilities that no other species share or is seen even capable of sharing.

Sometimes man is seen as contrasted with nature, in others, he is taken as part of nature. The difference is not trivially linguistic. To set man against nature is to emphasize his distinctiveness such as rationality, creativity and freedom, where as nature lack these attributes. To count man as part and parcel of nature emphasize the continuity of human, animal, organic and inorganic worlds and suggest that human behaviour may be amendable to the same kind of investigations that are effective in studying other domains of nature.

The relationship between man and nature is seen as inseparable. From the spiritual world outlook this is so because both of them are products of same God. Material world outlook also endorses this view; because everything in nature is made of the same stuff, namely, matter. The body of man is not only a part of nature but it is an "epitome of nature," a "microcosm."

Right from the Indo-Iranian period, many a general notion regarding the cosmic role of the natural elements like, water, fire and wind had come into being. Simultaneously, there also developed an idea of the correspondence between these elements and constituent principles of the body. The concepts of *ṛta* in the Vedas, which can be interpreted as a scientific concept of natural law or as a moral one, was the reflection of the primitive thought of man in regard to the intimate interaction between man and nature. Thus man and nature, and sometimes God also, appear in one-way or another in all the creative activities of man.

If we look at the human environment, the continuous interaction between organisms and surrounding is very evident. It can be often said that man, for more than any other animal, has developed the ability to modify environment and thus to live under a wide range of physical and biological conditions. He has, in fact, created a new "biome" or ecological formation — the man altered landscape, which is rapidly replacing other terrestrial landscapes as forests are cleared, grasslands and desert irrigated. Man assuming ecological dominance within this biome has effected directly or indirectly all other organisms living there; he has become a new geological force.

The environment in return effects man through biophysical limitations, behavioural controls and resource availability. Bio physically, human body can function properly only in certain suites of environmental conditions in terms of oxygen, heat, light, humidity and precipitation, etc. The survival of human body depends on the above factors. Various combinations of environmental factors have not only affected but conditioned human behaviour. Environment influences and conditions the thoughts, ideologies and culture of human being. Even the social, economic and political behaviour is influenced to certain extent by man's perception of environmental factor and his responses to these factors. Frequency and magnitude of extreme natural events and environmental factors like volcanoes, earthquake, floods, droughts, landslides, storms, etc., influence human perception of natural environment and decides his reaction and responses to these events. For example, the inhabitants of a particular region, which are largely adversely affected by recurrent floods, may thus conceive that rivers are sources of perpetual disasters. The most significant aspect of the environment in influencing human activity is the availability of resources.[10]

Man is an important part of the biotic component of the environment and simultaneously he is also an important factor of the environment. Thus man plays important roles in the natural environmental systems in different capacities such as "biological or physical man," "social man," "economic man," "technological man," etc. The role of most primitive "biological or physical man," in the functions of natural environmental system was fundamentally that of user of natural resources and thus he played the role of a factor of the environment but as the skill and technology of man developed with cultural development, his roles towards natural environment also changed progressively. The role changed from *user* through *modifier* and to *destroyer* of the environment. Modern technological man, intoxicated by highly advanced technology and materialistic viewpoints, has changed and is changing the environment for his vested

---

10. S.R. Joshi, N. Joshi, *Man and His Environment*, Shillong: Gautam Bros., 1999, pp. 16-17.

interests to such an extent that even the very existence of human beings is threatened.[11]

If we look at historical progression of man-environment relationship it becomes clear that purely natural relationship between "physical primitive man" and natural environment during pre-historic period has changed to hostile relationship between "technological man" and the environment at present. This substantial change and shift in the actions with the natural environment has given birth to numerous environmental problems of serious consequences because the changes effected by man in the natural environment have become unadjustable by the inbuilt self-regulatory mechanism of natural environ-mental system.

"Organism" and "environment" are seen as not contrasting or mutually exclusive terms; rather, they represent interacting systems, and the distinction is useful in analysis only when this is kept in mind. Environment is often viewed as contrasted over "nature versus nurture" in shaping human personality. There is no "versus." Every individual is the product of a certain genetic potentiality finding expressions in a particular environment or a series of environments. Biologist thus, avoids the dangers of looking at the living members of the community as separate from their surroundings.

When nature includes man, then it is seen as contrasted with the *supernatural*. The idea of supernature comes into existence from the allegedly miraculous events, events, which it is claimed, the power of law of nature could not

---

11. *Ibid.*, p. 17.

bring about. It is not so difficult to distinguish coherently between the concept of nature and the concept of super nature. The crucial distinction is that we can differentiate between what lies within the capacities of nature from what lies beyond them. Our knowledge of nature's powers and laws is itself derived from our experience and observation of the events. What we judge to be possible depends on what we have reasoned to believe actually occurs or has already occurred. We cannot assemble what we experience with the miraculous happenings, which we are unable to experience. To exclude the unknown events would be to imply that we already know what nature's powers are, that there are some criteria prior to experience by which we describe our observation. But to include them makes it impossible for us to treat them later as miraculous exceptions to natural laws.

Certainly it is not legitimate or valid to move from the statement, "this event is inexplicable in terms of our scientific knowledge of nature," to the statement, "this event must be a supernatural intervention." The scientist is by no means committed to claim that he has at any particular time, the concepts and theories for any explanatory task. Actually, he is constantly revisive and adding to these. We are not, therefore, forced to draw the conclusion that an event has a supernatural source on the grounds that it is inexplicable or anomalous in terms of present-day science. Indeed, it is only with the help of an independently established set of beliefs about God that one could plausibly interpret an event as supernatural.

Although it has been implied above that God must be conceived in contradiction to nature, this is true only if God is transcendent, not immanent, or if immanent than transcendent as well. To Pantheism, this distinction between nature and God is only the different views or aspects of the one and the same reality.

Charles T. Rubin feels the need to go a little deeper into the meaning of environment by driving home the socio-political aspects. He said, so called "Environmentalism" so pervades our outlook that we do not see it as an *ideology*, a particular set of beliefs.[12] And on the other hand, if we cast it as an *ideology*, it is likely to produce objections. Firstly, environmentalism will be said to be, not an ideology, but the most lucid common sense about the need to improve our relationship to the world around us. "Most people do not need a scientific panel to tell them that air is not supposed to be brown, that streams are not supposed to be concerned with raw sewage."[13] But this argument involves a deeper issue, as perceptions of environmental problems are many and deep.

For generations, what we now call substantial sanitation was simply considered a fact of life. It did not pose much as a problem until people began to think that something else was both possible and desirable. "Problems" come to exist when people can imagine that the world does not have to be the way it is, i.e., when they have a vision of the future

---

12. Charles T. Rubin, "Managing the Planet: The Politics of the Environment," in *Creation at Risk?: Religion, Science, and Environmentalism*, eds. Michael Cromartic, William B. Eerdmans (Michigan/Cambridge/U.K.: Publishing Company Grand Rapids), 1987, : 1-2.

13. As quoted in Charles T. Rubin, *Managing the Planet: The Politics of the Environment*, p. 2.

that is different from the past, and when they think they possess the power to bring the vision to life! Visions of this sort, of course, are such stuff as ideologies are made on.

Some says that "environmentalism" is a catch — all phrase for so many different points of view that it hardly achieves the internal coherence we associate even with loose use of the word "ideology" and bears no likeness, whatsoever, to a formal ideology. This is about the diversity of environmental visions. There are serious disagreements among various schools of thought about environmentalism. Those who think that population is the environmental problem, look askance at those who blame technology, those who focus on the problems that human beings create for themselves are criticized for a wrong-headed anthropocentricism by those who think we need to look first to the well-being of existence of some kinds of diversity. Of course this must not lead to the conclusion that environmentalists have no common assumptions.

People who believe that free and responsible human beings are best to live in harmony with nature call themselves "free market environmentalists." A great many of those relatively few and hardy souls who criticize the "environmental movement" for one reason or another do so having asserted that, whatever the weight of their criticism, they still consider themselves "environmentalists."

If so, then what are the common assumptions that are definitive of environmentalism? Charles T. Rubin argues that environmentalism is generally defined by a concern for man's relationship to nature that arises out of utopian and totalitarian political programmes for the complete reformation of human life on earth. He suggest that "environmentalism is utopian in the sense that the project it puts forward contains such tensions or internal contradictions that the goals sought either will never be achieved or, if achieved, will have harmful consequences."[14]

Again for those who view the environment not from totalitarian/holistic approach but instead addresses problems singly needed to include a rethinking of the usefulness of the term "environment."

We expect more of the environment in which we live, however, than conditions suitable for our health, resources to run the economic machine, and whatever is meant by good ecological conditions. We want to experience the sensory, emotional and spiritual satisfactions that can be obtained only from identification with the places in which we live. This interplay and identification generates the spirit of place. The environment acquires the attributes of place through the fusion of the natural and the human order. All human beings have approximately the same fundamental needs for biological and economic welfare, but the many different expression of humanness can be satisfied only in particular places.

An interesting angle to this discussion on nature lies in an answer to the question — can values be in any way derived from description of nature? Moral philosophy has handled debates on whether appeals to nature and the natural properly settle moral or artistic issues. Naturalistic ethical theories have suggested different answers to this. On the one hand, nature is seen as irreducibly complex, the theatre not of a simple cosmic process but of countless

---

14. *Ibid.*, pp. 3-4.

and diverse processes, and if processes have produced mind but are not themselves guided by intelligence, then there will be little plausibility in arguing directly from "natural' to "good' or "obligatory." On the other hand, where nature is taken as created by a wholly good, wise and omnipotent deity, to be natural is *prima facie*, to be worthy of being created by such a deity.

According to M. Bookchin

> Whatever nature may mean, we must determine in what way humanity "fits" into it. And we must confront the complex and challenging questions of the relationship of society more specifically, the different cultural forms that appeared in the past, that exist today, and that may appear in the future — to nature, unless we answer these questions with reasonable clarity — or at least fully discuss them — we will lack ethical directions in dealing with our environmental problems. Unless we know what nature is and what humanity's and culture's place in it is, we will be left with vague intuitions and visceral sentiments that neither cohere into clear views nor provide a guide for effective directions.[15]

Many years of research and concern over environment have produced very less precision on the question what is environment? Sometimes environmentalists even fail to define the term. And even when definitions are given, they differ on what is included or excluded. From this, it can be said that, the so-called environmental crisis is much rooted

---

15. Murray, Bookchin, *The Philosophy of Social Ecology: Essays on Dialectical Naturalism*, *op.cit.*, 1996, p. 3.

in its misconception of the very term "environment." Lynton Keith Caldwell, one of the architects of the National Environmental Policy Act, writes:

> There could be no greater misconception of its meaning than to believe it to be concerned only with endangered wildlife, human-made ugliness and pollution.[16]

This is a statement of profound significance. In essence, it implies that the present crisis of the environment is an outward symptom of an inner crisis of mind and spirit. So, calls for a spiritual renewal and our attitudes towards the *concept* of environment are welcome, but, as we will see, when they are driven by environmental necessity, they tend to take on a distinctly problematic cast.

It may be safely argued that environment is an inseparable whole and is constituted by the interacting systems of physical, bio-logical, climatic and cultural elements which are interlinked individually as well as collectively in myriad ways.

Let us now turn to the questions what is preserv-ation? What is to be preserved? Why it has to be preserve? And when does it come of preservation?

Scholars have paid little attention to the definition of preservation, to what it really means. On the other hand, philosophers have apparently accepted John Passmore's distinctions between "Conservationism" as the expression of anthropocentric motives and that the "preservationism" as the expression of non-anthropocentric motives. To

16. As quoted in Charles T. Rubin, *op.cit.*, p. 5.

conserve is to save. I shall use the word to cover only the saving of natural resources for later consumptions, where the saving is primarily a saving *from* rather than a saving *for*, the saving of species and wildernesses from damage and destruction, I shall speak, rather of preservation. Preservation is saving natural things for their own sakes.[17]

The *Encyclopedic Dictionary of Environment* has defined the term "preservation" in the following ways:

Keep in existence unchanged, natural resources, structures or situations which have been inherited from the past. [18]

So, environment preservation generally will mean the protection of a natural environment from any human activity for the sake of posterity.

The very concept of preservation entails that something in the natural environment is worth preserving and must be preserved. And, at the same time it answers the question as to why it has to be preserved as the very meaning of environment entails the surviving platform of life on earth. In other words, the physical environment has to be preserved because it is on the verge of collapse due to excessive human intervention in the form of industrialization, development and modernization.

When asked — why should we try to preserve our environment? The answer goes far beyond a desire to

---

17. John Passmore, *Man's Responsibility for Nature,* New York: Charles Scribner's Sons, 1974, p. 111.

18. *Encyclopedic Dictionary of Environment*, eds. G.R. Chhatwal, D.K. Pandey, K.K. Nanda, vol. III, New Delhi: Anmol Publication, 1988, p. 708.

preserve beauty of unspoiled, or natural areas, although this could be a very important reason. A popular explanation is that man needs to preserve the balance in nature, for if that is destroyed man will have no place else to go. We are now realizing that this vast network of chemical and biological interaction generates and preserves our soil and air, and maintains the purity of our water. We have seen that interrupting the process of energy flow and chemical cycling or changing the rate at which they occur can threaten the stability of our life-support processes at the local and in the long run at the global level.

There is the "aesthetic argument" whose primary appeal is to the beauty of nature and to the pleasures and solace afforded by an unspoiled environment. According to this argument nature should be preserved for the same reason we would want to preserve a work of art: because of the delight and inspiration it provides.[19]

In contrast with this is the argument from the "intrinsic worth" of nature. Nature should be preserved not as a means to any human end, whether aesthetic or utilitarian, but because it is inherently valuable as nature and in itself, because its value cannot be regarded as "reducible to its value to God or humanity."[20] Nature has value independently of human purposes or perception therefore, human being should revere it and as far as possible leave it as it is.

---

19. Sujata Miri, *Ethics and Environment: Theory and the Adi and Khasi Practice*, Guwahati, Delhi: Spectrum Publications, 2001, p. 23.
20. Robert Goodin, *Green Political Theory*, Oxford: Policy Press, 1992, p. 82.

We also have the argument from utility, which emphasize the importance of nature as a means of human survival. We have the duty to preserve the resources of nature because they are essential to all human life both now and in the indefinite future.

To the bio-centric philosophers such things as species, habitats, ecosystems and even the earth's bio-sphere as a whole are part of the moral community. So, they vehemently oppose the anthropocentric ethical theo-ries, which are not only mistaken as to the composition of the moral community, but also have contributed to the degradation of the environment by supporting the effect, the view that nature should be exploited to satisfy human needs intelligently.

Therefore, bio-centric philosophers believe that only if nature is included in the moral community — only if we recognize that we have a direct obligation to protect nature — will we succeed in preserving the environment.

We are now coming to a different spiritual and intellectual realization about the nature of our existence. The reductionists, atomists and materialists have dominated Science and Philosophy so long that we nearly exhausted the usefulness of those mindsets. We must respectfully bury the mindsets of Aristotle and Descartes in order to embrace a newer, more relevant grasp of the role of our existence. We know that a human being, or any other life form, is more than the sum of its mineral components. It is the dynamic interaction of those components that distinguishes us from the non-sentient. And all this is seen as a reason for us to protect and preserve our environment.

From the above discussion it is clear that nature is valued for its contribution to human well-being and survival. Most of the discussions in the philosophical literature centre on one or the other of these reasons for valuing nature. Even those who appeal to reasons of a different kind — for example, to aesthetic or therapeutic values found in nature — do not often regard historical associations as being relevant to judgements of worth.[21]

According to Janna Thompson, "among the reasons that people often give for preserving or valuing a natural landmark or environment is the claim that these things are part of the heritage."[22] The tree is valued because of its historical association with a community and not because of its beauty or rarity. Other natural objects or landscapes are valued because they have traditionally been celebrated as inspiring or beautiful, or it figures in the legends of the indigenous people of the area.

The idea that wilderness is part of the national heritage, a key to understand the history and character of people, is also a common theme in North American writings. It should be noted that wilderness is heritage in this sense not because

---

21. However, references to historical value do figure in some agreements to protect wilderness. For example, the U.S. Wilderness Act of 1964 refers to the historical value that wilderness may have. Something can count as World Heritage for either historical or ecological reasons and many areas so protected — like Kakadu National Park in Australia's Northern Territory — have this status because they are significant both for their natural qualities and their association with indigenous people and their culture.

22. Janna Thompson, "Environment as Cultural Heritage," *Environmental Ethics*, 22 (2000) : 241.

it was loved and appreciated by our forefathers, but because of its influence on the characters of the people of a nation. "American regarded wilderness as a moral and physical wasteland fit only for conquest and fructification in the name of progress, civilization, and Christianity."[23]

Although appeals to heritage of natural objects and environments are common, they have not been much discussed by philosophers. Some environmentalists are critical of these appeals because they are essentially human-centered. A landmark or environment is being preserved because of its human association, not because it is valuable in itself. However, even eco-centric environmentalists have pragmatic reasons for making their kinds of argument, and those environmentalists who are less convinced of the value or meaningfulness of eco-centric positions should welcome other ways of making a case for the value of nature for human beings. One of the problems with human-centered environmentalism is that the environments and natural objects that many people want to preserve are not always essentials to human survival or health. There seems to be a gap between our desire to preserve and what can be defended by human-centered arguments.

Nevertheless, many environmentalists are going to doubt whether arguments for the preservation of cultural heritage — mine or any other — can play a significant or helpful role in struggles for environmental preservation.

Historically, although the common ancestry of all life explained by the Darwinian theory of evolution offered

---

23. Roderick Nash, *Wilderness and the American Mind*, rev. edn., New Haven and London: Yale University Press, 1973, p. xv.

scientific encouragement to the views of life as an interdependent whole, it was only in the twentieth century, however, that calls[24] were made for the extension of the ethical concern to include all life on earth. Studies in the 1960s and 1970s of the destruction of the natural environment resulting from pollution, logging and fears that natural resources, such as fossil fuels, were being rapidly depleted, intensified calls for a re-evaluation of human attitude towards, and interaction with, the natural environment. Occasionally, apocalyptic visions of humanity acting as its own executioner by cresting a world inhospitable to life gave impetus and urgency even to the field of environmental ethics. Gradually, as the effects of rapid industrialization have become evident, emphasis has shifted from the study of nature to a desire to preserve it.

In the 1980s and 1990s environmentalism entered a new phase with governments in broad agreements over the seriousness of environmental problems. At the same time, environmentalists, social activists, and humanists, working through specific and often emblematic issues, seek to bring about a fundamental shift in perceptions of the environment and its preservation in the minds of the people.

Due to industrial development, deforestation, urbanization, population exploitation and neglect of nature has resulted in adverse condition and has jeopardized the natural existence of nature. Mankind through industrialization, pollution of air, water and soil has raped mother

---

24. I have in mind such calls that formulated by one of the founders of the wilderness society, Aldo Leopold, in his influential work *A Sand County Almanac* (1994), which is made for the extension of ethical concern to include all life on earth.

Earth mercilessly. The problems of pollution have posed the highest threat to human existence at present.

Generally pollution may be defined as the influx of extraneous materials in a particular environment in concentrations that are harmful to living organisms or plant life. The dictionary meaning of pollution is stated as:

> The process of polluting the water, air, atmosphere, etc., especially by means of poisonous chemicals. E.g., changes in climate due to pollution of atmosphere by industrial waste, environmental pollution."[25]

So-called environmental pollution is a matter of life and death. We who live and breathe, drink and eat, play and enjoy the bountiful gifts of nature today, must consider it our duty to leave this earth a cleaner and safer place to live. We must care for nature and then only nature will care for us. Men's very survival on this earth depends on his harmony with nature, as there is a close interaction between the two, i.e., mankind and nature. The human being who is also the creation of the nature must always keep this in his mind that his happiness will increase if he respects the nature but if he misuses, or overuses or abuses it, then it will imperil the very right to life.

Our environment in which we live and adapt ourselves in, would include not only the physical aspect but also the socio-cultural and biological aspects. It is evident that man's physical and mental health appears to be connected to his

---

25. John Sinclair (editor-in-chief), *Collins Cobuild English Lanuage Dictionary*, Birmingham: Collins Publishers, 1987, p. 1110.

symbiotic relationship with the ecological system in which we live. Therefore, it has to be preserved.

The fight against pollution has been on ever since when, emperor Ashoka issued edicts engraved on stones, ordering the protection of human health and the life of animals and plants, in the fourth century BC. But magnitude of the problems was less alarming in the earlier days and so the solutions were also less sophisticated. The world today has reached a point where we cannot put the clock back or resign ourselves to a simplistic natural state.

In order to minimize the effects of industrial pollution in degrading environment so much work has been done-solutions has also offered and so many are concerned to preserve the environment. In other words, the strategy and policies to preserve the environment are many and varied.

One-way of looking at this much talked about environmental preservation comes from the educationists. Their argument is that — much needs to be done to "educate' ourselves in preserving, appreciating and nurturing our natural sources to a more meaningful humane and civilized utilization. The knowledge of environment and environmental degradation can no more be the subject of specialists only. Time has come for the introduction of environmental study as a regular subject in schools. Such an involvement will lead to awareness for the preservation of nature, which has to touch the heart of every common man. This awareness will be our greatest "defence against pollution."

It is encouraging that many environmentalists are trying to preserve and restore environment. But one must also not neglect the fact that it is also our responsibility to feel the need for educating the people about the very importance of preserving it. Until and unless the mind of the people is enlightened about the very fact — the importance of environment; listening to an environment programme and planting a tree may not make much sense. There is a possibility that they listen and plant just because they are told so.

One can also argue that public action alone is not enough to preserve the environment; individual discipline for proper utilization is a fundamental need. Environmental degradation is a serious concern for human existence for which every concerned individual should focus with serious attention knowing that we are at the brink of total annihilation of our world.

In spite of many efforts, preservation of the environment still remains, by and large, a misunderstood subject. Most people are not aware of the fact that it is not mere protection of a few animals or plant species or planting of trees, or the concern over big polluting industries, or the simple cleaning up of the environment that constitute environmental preservation. It is a combination of all these.

Ecology shows us the importance of *diversity* in maintaining viable ecosystems. But when diversity becomes a good in itself, it functions as an ethical principle. An ecologically informed society preserves not only individuals as species but sees more importantly the goodness of the species, which cannot be realized apart from their having a place in a functioning ecosystem. Environmental ethics in which the biotic community is the center of values will not focus solely on the preservation of a particular species or on the maintenance of diversity, but on maintaining the webs of relationships that make up the components of ecosystems.

Thinking along the line Rene Dubos suggested that, "instead of being exclusively concerned with the nation or the world as a whole, they should first consider more local situations."[26] In a very down to earth and practical level we should first consider situations, which concern our day to day life decision and action. But such prosaic aspects of our lives are hardly worth mentioning from the perspective of the environment, yet they are essential to the quality of life as we live it day-to-day. If one view "the environment" from a down to earth perspective we come to understand that our relationship to the world around us is not something special that requires new environmental ethics or philosophies, but is just part of the ongoing quest to be decent human beings. Instead of aspiring to "save the earth" or "plan it for the planet" where only the experts deal with one should better opt for an environment preservation strategy in which every human being has a part to play and something which is even within the reach of the common people. Such problems, which we can identify in our relationship to that part of nature, that is well known and close to us can be addressed by individual efforts and by voluntary actions. If one see how important it is to maintain the freedom to clean up our own-backyards, then we will be less likely to think we are just doing our part to

26. As quoted in Charles T. Rubin, "Managing the Planet: The Politics of the Environment" in *Creation at Risk: Religion, Science and Environmentalism*, eds., Michael Cromartic, William B. Ecrdmans (Michigan/Cambridge: U.K. Publishing Company Grand Rapids, 1987, p. 15.

achieve some vision of a global utopia. Because it cannot be achieved by some movements or regulations that is forced upon from outside, if the one who acts with the nature do not improve that responsibility within him. If we do so, will conduce to a shared sense of individual responsibility, and not to the evasions that result when we define problems in such comprehensive terms that only a powerful, centralized government, organization can deal with them.

It is incumbent upon us to find better ways of managing the environment and to find new sorts of ethics that include all living creatures. Without this, the vision of a new society will be no more than an idle dream. One can boldly say that, the ills and profound frustration which have overtaken man are not merely due to industrial civilizations, inadequate planning and faulty execution, but are caused by fundamental errors in our basic thinking about goals.

But such an alternative and evaluative thinking about the environment does not require *living* differently. It is *knowing* differently. We must be able to provide a rational justification for our new lifestyles, which will amount to nothing less than providing a new rationality. We must be convinced in our hearts and mind that our frugality is not a depressing abnegation and self-denial but an act of positive manifestation of new qualities; only then will it become "elegant frugality" Therefore, alternative lifestyles must signify not only changes in our technology, economics and patterns of living, but also changes in our morality, rationality, and conceptual thinking.[27]

---

27. Henryk Skolimowski, *Eco-philosophy*, Boston/London: Ideas in Progress, 1981, pp. vii-viii.

Then, what is the factor, which promoted peoples to preserve the environment? It is the attitude of a human being towards nature. Attitude is based on the relationship between man and nature — what a person thinks of himself in relation to the things surrounding him and decides his attitudes. If a person thinks of himself to be a master he will rule over all other things. If he thinks to be at par he will know the pains of the other things and wish their well-being. Thus, man and nature relationship forms the main corpus in discussing environmental preservation. Therefore, while tracing this environmental preservation in different stream of thought I have concentrated on "Man" and "Nature" relationship in the next chapter.

3

Nature vs. Man

IN the face of the ecological crisis, *care* and *respect* for nature has become imperative. In this context man and nature relationship assumes greater relevance. Although human beings transcend nature in many respects, they are part of it in almost everything. One can even go further and say nature is part of us.

> To experience the world as an extended self and its story as our own extended story involves no surrender or eclipse of our individuality. In the first movement, our infancy as a species, we felt no separation from the natural world around us.[1]

Nature is respected as the mother of all beings, the foundational base of which is earth and its atmosphere. It is motherly in its whole behaviour, as the creatrix of all living beings, as a caring nurse, or as a sheltering hen, which tries to keep all beings under its protective wings. We humans, the wisest of all her creatures, are expected to know this familial function of mother earth and live in her lap, involving ourselves in her concerns with a deep sense of

---

1. Joanna Macy, *World as Lover, World as Self*, Berkeley: Parallax Press, 1991 p. 13.

solidarity with her and with all her other children, the creatures of this life-bearing planet. A rational and commonsensical understanding of the healthy relationship and interrelationship of our life in union and communion with these beings of nature is a must. As such an understanding may be defined as a rational, critical, evaluative and relational study of all living and non-living beings in their mutual inter-dependence and inter-relationship as well as their foundational connections with the law of nature.

The central question in Environmental Philosophy — "What kind of relationship should be between Man and Nature?" — has been viewed in two different ways. One view conceives of nature as an order that includes man, the second conceives it as an alien order from which Man is excluded.

It is Galileo (1564-1642) in the Western world who conceived of nature as a "mechanical system" which is to be managed and controlled.[2] The simplification that Galileo imposed on nature was significant in developing a highly potent science of prediction. For instance, if a simple ideal model can be found of the relationship between the distances covered by a falling body and the time during which it falls, and then one can predict at any future time exactly where the body will be. If the body does not fall precisely in accordance with that relation, the deviations may be explained by interfering factors such as friction, thus offering the possibility of further and more

---

2. Rachels, James & A. Frank, Tillman, *Philosophical Issues: A Contemporary Introduction*, New York: Harper & Row Publisher, 1972, p. 339.

accurate prediction. If an event in nature can be predicted then it can be controlled.

From the above it follows that the whole of nature is no longer intelligible to men, only the part that is amenable to mathematics. Nature, so delimited, is a blind, lifeless thing that could not possibly be the locus of values or have intrinsic worth. Thus, Man is viewed as an alien in this world, and his life of consciousness belongs to another order of things.

In sharp contrast to such a position stands Spinoza. According to Spinoza, the chief good of man is that he should arrive at the knowledge of the union existing between the mind and the whole nature. It is necessary to understand as much of nature as will enable us to attain the aforesaid character. For Spinoza, nature is the ultimate reality. His view is monistic in nature — that there is no place for dualism or plurality in the universe. All the variety and multiplicity found in the universe is due to the manifestations of one absolute reality in different forms. Nature according to him, includes all but excludes none. In this way, man is only a part of nature or rather he is only the manifested being of nature.

John Stuart Mill disagreed strongly with Spinoza's notion that what is morally good for man can begotten from a study of nature that reveals an ultimately harmonious unity which, once recognized, will enable us to live in beatitude. Mill says:

> To guide our actions by the analogy of the course of nature. No one, either religious or irreligious believes that the hurtful agencies of nature, considered as a whole, promote good purposes,

> in any other way than by inciting human rational creatures to rise up and struggle against them. All human action what ever, consists in altering, and all useful action in improving the spontaneous course of nature.[3]

Both the views of Spinoza and Mill have their own value about Man and Nature relationship. Man is a part of nature and should live according to the laws of nature. In other words, man derived his goodness from nature. The human conduct can be found in nature.

Science is a mechanism of discovery and control — there is no question about this. Our sciences yield knowledge of means, but not of human ends. Here, then, is our idea of man's relationship to nature. Man is within nature as an active, functional being. But his natural propensity is to control nature through transformative activities whose goals cannot themselves be ascertained in nature. Man is both within nature and without it. His relationship to nature is therefore distinctively dualistic. Thus, our enthusiastic efforts to control nature have produced an environment which possess a challenge to the continued existence of a science of control. And science is part of this environment.

Probably the dominant chorus within the modern scientific fraternity is that the cosmic process is a matter of chance and that the notion of purpose is a question of individual prediction. Richard Dawkins writes:

---

3. John Stuart Mill, "Nature" in J.H. Randall, Jr., Justus Buchler, Evelyn Urban Shirk, eds., *Reading in Philosophy* New York, 1950 p. 57.

> Natural selection, the blind, unconscious, automatic process which Darwin discovered, and which we now know is the explanation for the existence and apparently purposeful form of all life, has no purpose in mind. It has no mind. It does not plan for the future. It has no vision. If it can be said to play the role of a watchmaker in nature, it is the blind watchmaker.[4]

Steven Weinberg echoes the same when he say that we like to think that we are very special and that we are not the result of a series of accidents reaching back to the "Big Bang," but on the contrary something within the cosmic plan. We do not realize that this homely earth is a tiny part in a really hostile universe and is destined to perish in extreme cold or heat. "The more the universe seem comprehensible, the more it also seems pointless."[5]

We have now come to the awareness of the role that the modern scientific attitude played in the degradation of the environment. As a result, going beyond a mechanistic fragmented world-view, some trends of contemporary scientific theories have opened up a new world-view of oneness of the universe, which includes not only our natural environment but also our fellow human beings. Work of Fritjol is such an example. He wrote:

> I saw cascades of energy coming down from outer space, in which particles were created and

---

4. Richard Dawkins, *The Blind Watchmaker*, Essex: Longman Scientific & Technical, 1986, p. 5.

5. Steven Weinberg, *The First Three Minutes: A Modern View of the Origin of the Universe*, London: Harper Collins, 1993, p. 149.

> destroyed in rhythmic pubes; I saw the storms of the elements and those of my body participating in this cosmic dance of energy; I felt its rhythm and I heard its sound, and at that moment I knew that this was the dance of Shiva, the Lord of Dancers.[6]

Further, the gospel of unity and inter-connectedness is echoed in the words of Gary Zukav, who thinks that the Philosophy of Physics borders on the Philosophy of Buddhism, which is a philosophy of enlightenment. Zukav says that the vital aspect of the Enlightenment state is the experience of an all-pervading unity. "This" and "that" are no longer separate entities. They are different forms of the same thing. Everything is a manifestation of *that* which is beyond words, beyond even space and time.[7]

The question of nature as the ground of human value has become the centre of the modern thinkers, concern, a kind of locus around which all other considerations have been revalued.[8] The contentions is that the balance of nature is, a kind of ultimate value, it performs the organizational and governing function of an absolute without at the same time possessing absolute ontological status. It is a natural norm, not a product of human convention or supernatural authority. The answer to the

---

6. Fritjof Capra, *The Tao of Physics: An Exploration of the Parallels between Modern Physics and Eastern Mysticism*, New York: Bantam Books, 1988, p. XIX.
7. Gary Zukav, *The Dancing of Wu Li Masters: An Overview of the New Physics*, New York: Bantam Books, 1980, p. 281.
8. I have in mind thinkers like Paul Sear in his work, *Utopia and the Living Landscape*.

value question, then, from an ecological point of view, is this: human values are founded in objectively determinable ecological relations with nature. The ends, which are proposed, must be such as to be compatible with the ecosystem of nature. Human life is both social and natural and hence takes place within a frame-work of limitations.

Thus, the philosophical understanding that has emerged from a dissatisfaction with the technocratic approach addresses itself to a basically new concern: to develop an ecologically creative sensibility towards the environment, one that can serve in the highest ethical sense as a guide for human conduct and provide an awareness of their place in nature.

According to Naess, an abiding concern for the environment can emerge from a deepened and expanded sense of self, *self-realization* is the process of acquiring that deepened sense of self, which he calls the *ecological self*. He distinguishes between the narrow ego and the self. The self of a person according to him is that with which the person identifies. I may identify with my thoughts and feelings and also beyond the narrow ego, with my family, friends and my nation. Self-realization is the process of identifying with the whole ecosystem. A person who has so identified with this environment has realized the ecological self.[9]

He regards this process of identifying with living beings as a necessary prerequisite for compassion and sharing

---

9. Arne Naess, "Self-realization: An ecological Approach to Being in the World," *The Trumpeter*, 4, no. 3 (1981) : 39-40.

feeling. He takes this process of identification to parallel the process of maturation. Infants seem to have little capacity to identify beyond their narrow egos. As one grows one can expand the scope of one's identifications. From this it seems that identification is not an inborn instinct.

> The very extent to which Naess and other deep ecologists encourage us to extend our sphere of identification suggests that they take identification to also depend in part on one's will.[10]

Again those who have answered "yes" to the question — whether man is a part and parcel of nature have also believed that nature has an intrinsic value, that is to say, not all values come from humans; that value can exist independently of us; it is not merely something we bestow. While, those who see man as apart from nature, for example the materialist or instrumentalist, look on nature as a store-house of resources to be organized and used by people, as having no other value than the value some humans give it. There has been a tendency in the powerful tradition of Western science to promote such instrumental thinking about nature through a drive to achieve scientific mastery over the non-human world.

The argument that, since man is himself a part of nature, his inherent subjectivity vitiates all attempts to derive values from natural processes, seems to be labored. Here we find that morality has its ground in nature,

---

10. Eric H. Retain, "Deep ecology and the irrelevance of morality," *Environmental Ethics*, 18 : 414.

providing us thereby with the philosophical foundation for a new theory of man's relationship to nature capable of redirecting the vast thrust of our civilization along more stable ecological lines.

While discussing the man and nature relationship amidst environmental crisis, we are confronted with the ethical questions — should there also be an ethical response to environmental crisis — a response at the level of the individual conscience? Rather than regard environmental degradation as a technical problem, or a problem that can be solved by legislation, should we all begin to develop a conscience about the way we act on, in and with our natural environment? And if we do begin to develop a conscience about the natural world, will it be nature itself? Or will it be ourselves? It is true that most of us are concerned, about what's happening to the world, but is our concern a moral concern? What are the real grounds of this concern? Are we concerned about the human species exclusively or are we concerned about nature in a more inclusive sense. Is there a sense in which it might be morally wrong to destroy an animal species or a plant species, or a wilderness or an ecosystem, regardless of whether such destruction has any consequence for human being?

The answers which environmentalists and ethicists have offered to such questions are varied ranging from the approach of the so called "shallow ecologists," who think that nature exist more or less for the benefit of human beings and to the approach of the "deep ecologists," who maintain that we need to think in a completely new way about nature, even to the extent of granting rights to all wild living things.[11]

The claims of deep ecologists — especially the claim that nature has rights — cannot be sustained. Such an ethic is untenable if it is going to be based on the belief that nature has rights or interests that can be represented, it should be in terms of our own interests and values as human beings; and if we are going to call this an ethical concern, it can only be on the basis that damaging the environment sometimes involves cruelty to sentient creatures, and puts the life and health of future generations of human beings at risk.

It is legitimate to think, therefore, that what we need is not so much a new environmental ethic. What we need is an outlook which is as fully appreciative of the natural world as is consistent with our need to survive in it, and which registers horror at any activity which cause the needless destruction of non-human species.

> "Man", currently so unfulfilled and divided against itself, has scarcely realized its potentialities, (to the extent of effecting the environment) takes a number of forms; a logically ambiguous "biocentrism" and of less strident anti-humanism are not set against "anthropocentrism" and humanism presumably the cardinal sins of an abstract "man", who is determined to despoil

---

11. Arne Naess "Deep Ecology and Ultimate Premises," *Society and Nature* 1 No. 2 (Sept./Dec. 1992). Also see, Arne Naess, "Deep Ecology in Good Conceptual Health," *The Trumpeter*, 3, 4 (Fall 1986); 20.

> an equally abstract "Nature". As a result, a simplistic biologism emerges, often structured around "Natural laws", that sees "Man" with ecological degradation. As a result, some voices in the ecology movement call for a moral biospheric democracy, in which humanity's "right" to live and fulfill itself is equitable with that same "right" in insects, beasts, and yes — Pathogenic viruses and germs.

Biocentrism is an effort to bridle "human" arrogance towards other life-forms and defy the present destruction of the biosphere. But how long one can continue to belabour "humanity" for its affront to the biosphere without distinguishing between rich and poor and exploiters and exploited, is a nagging problem that many environmental philosophers have yet to restore, or perhaps even recognize.

Ethicists had settled on at least one conclusion, as ethics become modern in Darwin's century: That the moral has nothing to do with the natural. Science describes natural history and natural way; ethics prescribe human conduct, moral law; and to confuse the two makes a category mistake, commits the naturalistic fallacy.[12] Nature simply is, without objective value; the preference of human subjects establish value, and these human values, appropriately considered, generate what ought to be. Nature is a moral; only humans are ethical subjects and objects of duty.

---

12. The expression "Naturalistic fallacy" was coined by G.E. Moore (1903) for the attempt to define the concept of Good.

Unsettled now, in the decade in which the current interest in man's relationship to nature emerges from a concern over the ecological dislocations, ethicists face foreboding revolution. Only the human species contain moral agents, but perhaps conscience of earth ought not to be used to exempt every other forms of life from considera-tion, with the resulting paradox that the sole moral species acts only in its collective self-interest towards all the rest.

> There is something over specialized about an ethic, held by the dominant class of *Homosapiens*, that regards the welfare of only one of several millions species as an object and beneficiary of duty. Without denying the duties within culture, this biological world that is also ought to be; we must argue from the natural to the moral.[13]

Faced with revolution, ethical conservatives may shrink back and refuse to think biologically, to naturalize ethics in the deep sense. They will fear that it is logically incoherent to suppose that there is non-anthropogenic value, or that this is too metaphysically speculative, ever to be operational. They will insist that it does not make any pragmatic difference anyway, claiming that an adequate environ-mental ethic can be anthropogenic, even anthropocentric.

---

13. Holmes Rolston III, "Challenges in Environmental Ethics" in *The Environment in question: Ethics and Global issues*, eds. David E. Cooper and Joy A. Palmer, London and New York: Routledge, 1992, p. 135.

When we face up to the crisis, however, we undergo a more direct moral encounter. Environmental ethics is not a muddle; it is an invitation to moral development. The ethics seeks an appropriate respect for all life.

> What ethics is about, in the end, is seeing outside your own sector of self-interest, of class interest. A comprehensive ethic will find values in and duties to the natural world.[14]

Environmental philosophers frequently differ over whether the proper motivation for environmental concern is love of nature or concern for human good. Subsequently, in the history of ecology, we find a struggle between two parallel views: one dedicated to the discovery of intrinsic value and its preservation and the other to the creation of an instrumentalized world and its exploitation.

What is significant in the later view is that it gave a mechanistic answer to the question of what nature is and what it ought to be. So, it chose to ignore any aspect of nature that could not fit into this mechanical picture. This mechanization of the modern world-view did not remain restricted to physical sciences. Environmental philosophers too were influenced and misleaded to take its thinking along with its utilitarian bias toward nature.

The environmental philosophy of domination in the West has been defended for it is regarded as necessary to carry out the law of progress. An aggressive (even violent) force of culture was in the offing to harness and subdue

---

14. Holmes Rolston III, *Challenges in Environmental Ethic*, 1992, p. 136.

the "savage." So, in such a set up, civilization is viewed as a declaration of independence from the natural world and the savage's cultural declaration.

In such a world-view, the exercise of reason over nature sounds highly ethical — as man's dominance over nature is justified as its sacred duty to live apart from the other creations on the bases of his "divine spark." Given such a world-view, preservation then, become a process of modification by collaborated force.

Unfortunately, there is a widespread skepticism among those with deep commitments to the natural world about the idea that humans can improve upon nature. While it seems obvious that humans can alter nature to better serve human uses, it is far from clear that humans can improve nature in non-utilitarian ways.

According to Barry Commoner, "Nature knows best" is the third law of ecology.[15] The gravity of his claim is underlined by its ranking with the first two: that everything is inter-connected, and that nothing is ever destroyed, only recycled. But this law is curiously normative, implying that humans, in their *valuing* of nature, ought to *follow* nature. Doing so is often a matter of prudence, but perhaps value in nature also generates human duties toward it. Perhaps in some ways nature even educates our character.[16]

---

15. Barry Commoner, *The closing circle: Nature, Man and Technology*, New York: Knopf, 1972, p. 41.
16. Holmes Rolston III, *Environmental Ethics*, Philadelphia: Temple University, 1988, p. 32.

But there are dissenting voices. John Stuart Mill exclaimed, "conformity to nature has no connection whatever with right or wrong."[17] William James called us to "the moral equivalent of war" in our human resistance to a moral nature:

> visible nature is all plasticity and indifference, a moral multiverse. And not a moral universe. To such a harlot we are no allegiance; with her as a whole we can establish no moral communion and we are free in our dealing with her several parts to obey or to destroy, and to follow no law but that of prudence in coming to terms with such of her particular features as will help us to our private ends.[18]

Everything conducted in accordance with the laws of nature — "follows nature" in a broad, elemental sense, and it is sometimes asked whether human conduct ought to follow these laws. In their cultural life, humans are not entirely subject to the laws of evolutionary nature. But humans are in a still more basic sense, subject to the operation of these natural laws that they sometimes seem to exceed. If nature is defined as the aggregate of all physical, chemical and biological processes, there is no reason why it should not *include* human agency.

---

17. John Stuart Mill, "Nature" (1874), in collected works Toronto: University of Toronto Press, 1963-77, 10 : 374-402, citation on p. 400.

18. William James, "The Moral Equivalent of War," in *Memories and Studies*, New York: Longman, Green, 1911 267—96.

In any case, when humans operate as agents on the world, we certainly do so by using rather than exempting ourselves from laws of nature. No one has ever broken the laws of gravity, or those of electricity, nutrition, ecology or psychology. All human conduct is natural inasmuch as the law of nature operate in us and on us willy-nilly. We can not help but follow nature, and the advice to do so in this is trivial, even while some high-level questions about the role of human deliberation in nature remain open.

Earlier ethical norms were concerned only with man's relations to others of his own kind. But in the recent years, men own well-being requires that the circle of co-operative communal relatedness be extended to encompass all beings. As a result, the ethical question has been posed more emphatically than ever. The conservationist movement is seen as grounded not only in science but also in a moral philosophy of interdependence and tolerance.

It is obvious that the nineteenth-century thinkers were a guest for a lost pastoral haven, for a home in an inhospitable and threatening world. They emphasized on the unpleasant aspect of modernity. There was also a felt need to restore a personal relation of man to the world around him and through that to the world of God. While there was the downright rejection of science as responsible for the alienation of men from nature as well as God, there was an attempt to spiritualize science by replacing the physico-chemical explanation of life and consciousness with a creative, unpredictable organizing energy inherent in all organisms.

The "holistic" movement aiming at the rejection of technological society, tried to blend science more fully into the whole fabric of human values instead of working as narrow specialization with elaborate instruments of measurement which it felt were the causes for the alienation of mankind generally from nature in the first place.

Ecologists have demanded that scientists these days are in danger of ignoring the whole complex of nature, the quality of organic inter-relatedness that defies analysis by the physicist or chemist. Along with this are mixed reactionary appeals to an earlier time when man's economy worked in harmony with nature.

The age of ecology has recovered the organic idealist's or mystic's delight in discovering the oneness of life behind the multiplicity of appearance. The new ecologists view ecology as a means to review the long lost fellowship and intimacy between man and other living beings. The ideas of man's autonomy can only be a delusion; man must accept the fact of interdependence and practice a life-revering ethic.

> The ecological approach leads to an understanding of the fundamental unity of humanity and nature — if, instead of seeing nature as separate from humanity, we see humanity and nature as one matrix, then it is clear that we are a part of nature. From the ecological perspective, it follows that conceptualizing humanity as "outside of" or "apart from" nature is an error.[19]

---

19. Andrew Mc Laughlin, "Images and Ethics in Nature," *Environmental Ethics*, 7 (1985) : 312-13.

Numerous questions of epistemology and ethics must repose within the context of the integration of humanity and nature. However, man really evolves a naturalistic ethic, or proposes how it might be evolved.

Today's ecological crisis is asking us to rethink our relations to other forms of life, and responsibilities towards the ecosystem. Many in the Green Movement for instance have criticized Western instrumental rationality as responsible for abusive and alienating exploitation of the environment and its other life forms and have argued that its scientific approach must yield to a more proper sense of our actual dependency on the ecosystem and of our organic ties and affinities with the earth and its various species. The ecologists tend to invoke nature as a domain of intrinsic value; truth or authenticity while environmentalists in the urban settings do occasionally make claims about the human feelings for nature and talk of the preservation of the beauty of nature (as opposed to the utilitarian approach). There are few who wish to conserve it as an intrinsic value. Those who wish to save the forest, etc., from human intrusion are few and far between today.

Human intervention into nature is inherent and inevitable. To argue that this intervention should not occur is utterly obfuscatory. What is important is whether man's practice is consistent with an objective environmental ethics that is sensibly evolved, not haphazardly rational, felt, or intuited. A humanity that failed to see that it is potentially nature rendered, the self-conscious and self-reflectious would separate itself from nature morally as well as intellectually.

> Ultimately there must come a recognition that the environmental crisis is a confrontation between man and nature; between human system whose influence is now global, and the natural ecosystem that have built and maintained the biosphere as a place suitable for life.[20]

For any one the beginning must come with some appreciation of man's place in the scheme of things, of his place in the global ecosystem.

Man must somehow see himself as the instrument of nature's own purpose, which his science must device and follow. Perhaps, in a new and more significant sense we shall have to revive the ancient exhortation to live *successfully, satisfactorily and virtuously*. But that does not mean that we must revert to what is adequately understood, the general direction of evolution will be more clearly seen, and human action and policy can then be properly aligned and assimilated to it.

Jim Cheney investigates the function of placc in the construction of our understandings of self, community and the world. He develops the idea of a *bioregional narrative*[21] (an environment ethic based on understanding of place in the context of our lives). The post-modernist account of ethics as "bioregional narrative" owes much to meditation

---

20. George Woodwell, "Science and the Gross National Pollution", in editorials of *Ramparts* Magazine, Eco-Catastrophe, San Francisco, California, Canfield Press (A Development of Harper & Raw), 1970, pp. 67-72.

21. Jim Cheney, "Post Modern Environmental Ethics: Ethics as bioregional narrative," *Environmental Ethics*, 2 (1989) : 13-20

on the role of land in tribal discourse. Tribal cultures have recognized the centrality of the land to the construction of self and community identities.

Inadequate attention has so far been paid to philosophical reflection on the bases of environmental concern, that is, on the conception of the relation between human beings and nature. "Shallow" and "Deep" eco-philosophies offer opposite ways of solving the tormented relationship between human beings and nature. Shallow ecologies, here called "environmentalist" philosophies, hold an anthropo-centric point of view and attribute to nature an instrumental value. Deep ecologies, here called "ecologist" philosophies, instead take on eco-centric point of view, that of the biosphere, and claim for nature an intrinsic value.

A little discussion about "shallow" and "deep" ecology, I find appropriate here. This distinction was first made by Norwegian environmentalist and philosopher Arne Naess who defined a shallow ecologist as anyone whose concerns are confined to his fellow humans and to a narrow selection of non-human forms of life, mainly those which serve human purposes.[22] What we need instead, in Naess's view, is an attitude of "respect for nature," which will not be centred on human interest alone.

Generally, a shallow eco-philosopher (or humanistic eco-philosopher, as many prefer to call it)[23] may be

22. Arne Naess, *Ecology, Community, and lifestyle*, Cambridge: Cambridge University Press, 1989, p. 29.

23. I had in mind thinkers like T.L.S. Sprigge in his Art. "Some Recent Positions in Environmental Ethics Examined." *Inquiry*, 24 (1991) : 107-128.

understood as one who is concerned at the pollution of our environment and the exhaustion of resources, at the destruction of rain forest and so forth. While his concern is solely with the threats to human welfare now and in future generation posed by such things. For such philosophers, nature matters as a resource for human needs, not as having some value independent of what there is in it for humans.

Even if deep ecologists of different times may use a language, which is different from that used by Naess, there are certain basic intuitions that mark off the deep ecologists as a group from their critics and opponents. One of their basic intuitions is that our dominant ethical codes and philosophies, especially Western codes and philosophies, have been too concerned with how we treat other human beings and not concerned enough with how we should treat non-human beings, including animals, plants and nature generally. Thus, to value other species ethically will mean a complete revolution in human attitudes. It will mean overcoming thousands of years of speciesism. It will mean valuing other species for their own sakes, treating them as ends in themselves, rather than merely as means to human ends. If a species of animal or plant is to be preserved, it should be preserved for its own sake and not just for the sake of the human species. This is an even more radical position than it seems. It means that non-human species should be regarded as having a right to exist, a right not to be damaged or polluted or destroyed. The recognition of such a right would mean the advocacy of a new environ-mental ethic, a nature-centered moral code that would make it immoral to always place human interests before the interests of the rest of nature, especially wild nature.

The deep ecologists are critical of any form of environmentalism that is not nature-centered. They regard any form of environmentalism that is human-centered environ-mentalism as shallow — shallow, because it will tend to value wild species, wilderness, and eco-systems only to the extent that they serve human needs and interests. In the view of the deep ecologist, to perceive anything as exploi-table or usable is already to perceive it unethically. The deep ecologist believes that nature must be respected as valuable in itself, regardless of its usefulness to human beings, regardless of its beauty or ugliness, regardless even of its interest to naturalists or scientists. The natural world is to be perceived as intrinsically or inherently valuable and not merely as instrumentally valuable.

The deep ecologists will agree with the shallow ecologists over many aspect but will also contend that some aspects of wild nature should be preserved, and protected against exploitation, although the net benefit for man, even including all forms of human enjoyment of wild nature, is thereby less than it might otherwise have been. The distinctive mark of the deep eco-philosopher, then, is that he thinks many things in nature besides, humans and animals are morally considerable and perhaps that nature itself, in some sense or other, is so as a whole.

The distinctions between deep and humanistic eco-philosophy are, none the less, certainly of philosophical interest. And perhaps they are of real practical interest too. For, it makes a real difference to the style in which conser-vationism may be defended, suggesting rather different responses to attacks from thoroughly anti-ecological quarters. As such, practically different policies will follow from differing views as to whether the wilderness or the species is worth preserving, not for human enjoyment, but in some sense for its own sake.

Andrew Brennan in his *Thinking about Nature,* attempts to provide a rational basis for the same general type of position as that of the deep ecologists related to what he thinks a better account of the upshot of ecology as a science. He calls his own position *ecological humanism.*[24] It is meant to fall between the extremes of merely shallow ecological ethics and deep ecological ethics.

The spirit of ecological humanism seems to lie in the claim that the identity of human beings, individually and as a race, is, in large part, a matter of their place in the larger bio-system, and that, therefore, the human good is not separable from the good of that system. Therefore, in order to preserve and promote the goods of human life we must concern ourselves with the needs of nature as something intrinsically bond up therewith. Thus, the humanistic ecologist's concern with nature is neither that of the shallow ecologist who sees it as merely an extrinsic means to human welfare, nor that of the deep ecologist who attributes to it in addition its own intrinsic value, but rather that of one who sees the value of each human life

---

24. Andrew Brennan, *Thinking about Nature : An Investigation of Nature Value and Ecology*, London/New York: Routledge, 1988, pp. XIII, 133.

as inseparable from its natural origins and basis.

Such a contention seems promising but is not, perhaps, altogether clear and is criticized by many thinkers. For it is argued that the claim about the identity of a human being, and of the human race generally, depends on its place in nature, is ambiguous.

Paul Taylor in his *Respect for Nature*, comes up with the idea of what he calls a *bio-centric ethic* of respect for nature.[25] This ethic is seen contrasted with what he calls a human ethic, in which concern is limited to the behaviour of humans towards each other. Taylor is of the contention that, we should recognize the bio-centric ethic and the humanistic ethic as two equally legitimate ethical pers-pectives, appropriate for approaching different questions. However, since they often conflict, we must try to find principles, which will mediate between them when necessary, and Taylor tries to develop these. However, the main concerns are to explain, what the bio-centric ethic, taken apart from the humanistic ethic, requires of us.

> The bio-centric ethic is an ethic of respect for wild living-things. It sees each living thing as of intrinsic value, indeed of equal intrinsic value, and requires of those who live by it that they attach equal importance to the achievement of what is good for it on the part of every single living thing.[26]

---

25. Paul Taylor, *Respect for Nature: A Theory of Environmental Ethics*, Princeton, N.J: Princeton University Press, 1986, pp. IX, 329.
26. See T.L.S. Sprigge, "Some Recent Position in Environmental Ethics Examined," *Inquiry*, 34 (1991) : 107-28.

This bio-centric ethic is by definition not concerned with respect for the inherent worth of living beings in general, but with that of wild living beings. However, Taylor acknowledges that a more complete moral position would have to cover the ethic of the bio-culture too, that is, the moral respect due to such non-human life as has become part of human civilization, e.g., farm animals, and plants cultivated for food, clothes and in gardens or parks. However, he does seem to think that the wild deserves a special respect simply as such.

Taylor bio-centric ethic has at its core the belief that every living thing is "a unified system of organized activity, the constant tendency of which is to preserve its existence by protection and promoting its well-being." As such, it has its own good which it is better that it should realize than fail to realize, and reflection shows that every living thing has equal, or rather an identically absolute, inherent worth, i.e., it is no more and no less important for one living thing (be it animal, plant, or even bacterium) to reach its good than another.

Deep ecologists usually hold a holistic ethic, which stresses the importance of *communities* of individuals, rather than of individuals.[27] Taylor's bio-centric ethic, in contrast, is explicitly not holistic. Respect for Nature, on his account, is respect for the inherent worth of each

---

27. This note is sounded by many deep ecologists. See, for example, John Rodman. "The Liberation of Nature," *Inquiry* 20 (1977) : 89. Kenneth. "From Egoism to Environmentalism," in K.E Goodpaster and K.M. Sayre, *Ethics and the Problems of the 21st Century*, Notre Dame: University of Notre Dame Press, 1979.

individual living thing and its claim to have its pursuit of its own good respected.

On the other, Holmes Rolston, differs, however, in his determined *holistic approach*. He is at one with Taylor in believing that every organism has its own good which matters to it, and should be taken account of by us, whether it is sentient or not.

> Kant knew something about others, but the only others he could see were other humans, others who could say "I". Environmental ethics calls for seeing non-humans, for seeing the biosphere, the Earth, ecosystem communities, fauna, flora, natural kinds that cannot say "I" but in which there is formed integrity, objective value independent of subjective value.[28]

However, Rolston differs from Taylor (as the quotation indicates) in that he thinks the most important values which an environmental ethics should teach us to recognize do not exist at the level of individuals but at the level of species and eco-systems. Although the good of an individual matters somewhat in itself, it matters much more as a phase either in the life of the species to which it belongs or the ecosystem.

> Life is a sacred thing, and we ought not to be careless about it. This applies not only to life with the capacity for experience, but to the lesser zoological and the botanical species. Individuals

---

28. Homes Rolston III, *Environmental Ethics: Duties to and values in the Natural World*, Philadelphia: Temple University Press, 1988, p. 340.

> have their intrinsic worth, but particular individuals come and go, while that wave of life in which they participate overlaps the single life span millions of times.[29]

Thus the preservation of species matters in itself and not simply as an object of interest to humans, or as somehow useful for humans. And the reason it matters is not just because humans find such a species something they enjoy wondering at. For wonder, if it is not misplaced, is at something, which has value in itself. Rolston's general idea is that a proper ethic will be based upon sensitivity to all these different sorts of value and will involve some attempts to act in ways, which harmonize the requirements laid down by each.

Now, we will turn to the shallow ecologist respond to the arguments of their deeper brethren. A recent critic of deep ecology has been the Australian philosopher John Passmore. Nothing is to be gained, in Passmore's view, by insisting that human beings share a moral community with the rest of nature:

> Bacteria and human beings do not recognize mutual obligation, nor do they have common interests. In the only sense in which belonging to a community generates ethical obligation, they do not belong to the same community. To suggest, then that exist, is to create confusion. The idea of "rights" is simply not applicable to what is non human.[30]

---

29. *Ibid.*, p. 309.

30. John Passmore, *Man's Responsibility for Nature*, 2nd edn., London: Duckworth, 1980, p.116.

He is not assured that there is anything evidently right about preserving biological diversity or anything evidently wrong with destroying a whole species. It all depends, he thinks, on the species.

In Passmore's perspective, the core concept of morality, such as the concept of rights, do not apply to something called nature. Animals and plants, either individually or collectively, do not recognize mutual obligations; do not participate in the moral community. The claims that it is intrinsically wrong to cut down a tree, or clear a wilderness, or even destroy a species of animal or plant, is "merely ridiculous." It is ridiculous because it introduces a concept of morality, which is barely intelligible to us, as if new moralities are the kinds of things that can be devised at will.

According to Passmore, calling for a new morality, for the recognition of the intrinsic worth of all living things, is like calling spirits from the vasty deep. To him, it sounds fine and worthy but ultimately it is an in-effectual gesture. New moralities cannot be conjured out of the air anymore than spirits from the vasty deep. A morality can only grow out of existing practices, values, and attitude of mind: as an extension or development of them. People who are concerned about the environment are therefore better off working with and within the value systems that already exist in whatever cultural and ethical tradition they find themselves. For example, the idea of reverence for life, which is promoted in the writing of some environmentalists is best understood as the development of an idea which is to be found in traditional religious and ethical thinking, namely, the idea of reverence for *human life*. It can be linked most specifically to the tribals' principle that it is wrong un-necessarily to destroy.

The reverence for non-human life which is demanded by deep ecologists can be seen as an extension of the sort of reverence which people already feel for historical or cultural artefacts like works of art, monuments or great buildings. This reverence is nothing radically new — it is embodied in the concept of "vandalism." And, such a concept of vandalism is seen extended to the things that are as old as the earth itself. And can also endorse taboo against the needless destruction of natures' own antiquities, namely, wild species and wilderness. As Passmore says,

> the man who cuts his name on a redwood is being a vandal, just as much as the man who scratches his initials on the portico of wells Cathedral.[31]

Thinking along in these lines, shallow ecologists go a long way with the deep ecologist — but they give different reasons for what they are doing. They advocate respect for nature, not because nature has rights, or has inherent worth or a good of its own, but because such an attitude is consistent with living a rational, moral and human life. Their contention is that by destroying aspects of nature we risk our own health and the health of future generations, and also debase ourselves by being destructive, cruel, or simply in sensitive.

We now have the essentials of two forms of ecological ethic — the question is — what shall we think about its claims?

---

31. John Passmore, *Man's Responsibility for Nature*, p. 125.

The deep ecologist will argue that the shallow approach is unethical because it is not nature-centred — that we should have the same respect for nature that we have had traditionally for the human species. There is one major problem, however, with this sort of claim. It does not seem possible to model our relationship with nature on the relationship we have with each other as members of the same species. It is not because morality involves some degree of mutual recognition of obligation, but because a nature-centered environmental ethic would require us to relate to our environment in ways, which would, on the face of it, make our own natural lives impossible. It is precisely because of our biological creativity, animal nature that we cannot respect (the rest of) nature in the way that we may respect each other.

Of course, we must control and manage all of this pollution, but it is not possible for us to opt for zero-pollution, zero-waste, zero-consumption, or zero-destruction (in the way that we can opt for zero-murder or zero-dishonesty. To put it another way, it is not possible for us to opt for absolute conservation or absolute respect for each other's lives or absolute honesty). To opt for absolute preservation would mean never making use of any part of the natural world, or seeing any part of it as a resource. If we treated everything in nature as an end in itself we could not justify our own survival, or for that matter the survival of other living species, since all living species survive and flourish at the expense of some members of some other species, whether it be other animal species or species of plant life.

I am inclined to think; therefore, that what is important is not the question of shallow or deep ecology. What we need is a concern that is evaluative enough to make us value the natural diversity of the world.

The entire biosphere should be cherished, and that its beauty, stability and integrity should be preserved for its own sake. People are usually ready to recognize that it should be cherished in the interests of humanity, including future generations; while some would add in here the interests of other species, as all these too depend on its preservation. Besides this instrumental basis (which may not call for the biosphere to be preserved exactly as it is), others attach to it aesthetic and sometimes religious value, and some regard it as a living organism, "Gaia," with an interest in self-maintenance and an intrinsic value of its own.[32]

Rodman hold further that ecosystems behave sufficiently like organisms to have interest of their own.[33] It would not be claimed that they have either desires or inherited capacities; the usual prerequisites of interests, but it would be suggested that they have an interest in the fulfilment of such inbuilt purposes as self-regulation and self-preservation. Intrinsic value would be ascribed here on the same basis.

---

32. See J.E. Lovelock, *Gaia: A New Look at Life on Earth.*

33. John Rodman, "Four Forms of Ecological Consciousness Reconsidered," in Donald Scherer and Thomas Attig (eds), *Ethics and the Environment* Englewood Cliffs, New Jersey: Prentice-Hall., 1983, 82-92.

Much of the same applies to such *non-living natural entities* as rivers, mountains and landscapes. There is a strong human interest in their preservation, which has aesthetic, intellectual and spiritual grounds, as well as a practical basis such as the interest in flood prevention and in fishing. Some people, however, would find here not only an instrumental value, dependent on the interests of living creatures, but also a non-derivative, independent interest consisting, for example, in the fulfilment of a river's self-scouring capacity.[34]

Besides their instrumental and aesthetic value, plants are sometimes held to have interests of their own, and this leads some to claim that their flourishing (involving, for example, growth to maturity) has a non-derivative value. This is not the sense of "interests," which relates to the satisfaction of desires or purpose, but one involving the development of the inherited capacities of a creature's natural kind.[35]

But whether or not such priorities are to be upheld, much of the most persistent and widespread argument for their preservation is an instrumental one. The impact of changes to *natural systems* could be colossal; and, even if a holistic view is rejected about the supposed intrinsic value of such systems, there is a growing understanding (exemplified in some of the above arguments) of the need

---

34. Robert H. Socolow, "Failures of Discourse: Obstacles to Integration of Environmental values into Natural Resources Policy" in Scherer and Attig, *ibid.*, pp. 152-69.

35. Robin Attfield, "The Good of Trees," *Journal of Value Inquiry*, no. 15 (1981) : 35-54.

for a holistic understanding of those natural networks on which all life depends. These systems, most people hold, matter because of the lives, which they support, rather than for what they are in themselves; but this is already to acknowledge the strongest of imperatives to preserve them.

However, another conception has arisen which complicates more radically the relation between nature and men. This view emerged with the conception, in the mid-nineteenth century, of the idea of evolution. Henceforth, nature could not be regarded simply as a machine, but was conceived as a process of continuous development. Laws of mechanics are reciprocal and reversible, but an evolutionary process is unidirectional and progressive. Further under this conception of nature, man is recognized as a product of evolution to nature, now comes to be envisaged in terms of that between organism and environment. The effect of this modification was not immediate or total, although its implications were revolutionary. Environment, at least in the first instance, was still regarded as external and set in opposition to the organism, which must adopt itself to alien conditions in order to survive. Man's adaptation follows upon that of lower species, which involves the development of sensibility, sense-organs for distance reception and cognitive apparatus. His capacity to know and to act intelligently, his conquest and control of nature, his social and technical advance, are thus seen as aspects of his adaptation to environment.

As the biological science and the study of ecology advances, it has become obvious that the idea of adaptation of organism to environment was a misconception, for the environment is not static, nor is it a mere external setting for indwelling life. Evolutionary change involves the environment equally with the living thing. The two constitute a single organic whole, an open system in dynamic equilibrium. Modification of or "control" over, the environ-ment, therefore, becomes less a means than a menace to human survival, and the exploitation of nature more inimical than advantageous. Voices are then raised advocat-ing conservation; but that involves a conflict between the demands of technical progress already made and those of environmental preservation. In the same sense, the demand is for a reverse of the evolutionary process, which runs counter to the very concept of evolution itself. The use of technology to mitigate the ravages of technology is severely limited. The preservation of resources; pollution of atmos-phere and water can be limited by new devices, but not eliminated. If population can be controlled, consumption may be limited, but the demand for progress and "develop-ment" will persist. The evolutionary process cannot be arrested and if social progress could not be reversed, it is not obvious that the result would be beneficial.

In the larger part of the Western history, nature as a physical place, which is also currently the dominant one — has been subordinate to the others. The basic understanding of nature today derives from the Romantic "nature poets" of the late eighteenth and early nineteenth centuries, who took nature to mean, in Raymond William's phrase, "what man has not made, though he made it long enough ago — a hedgerow or a desert — it will usually be included as natural."[36] Nature in this sense is usually thought of in tandem with "poetry," "lover" and "conservation."

Later, by the fifth century in Greece, a personified nature (Natura) had become an object of piety in its own right, endowed with a moral purpose and meaning, independent of mankind. Nature was also personified as the creative force within the universe — the immediate cause of phenomena. At times, the ancient Greeks personified nature more explicitly in female form, a practice still evident in our invocation of "mother Nature." These are the origins of a singular, capitalized nature, indicating how closely nature as essence or principle is related to nature in the plural as the totality of matter.

Nature is in some senses an irrevocable dictate: we have little choice but to respond to "the call of nature." Nature is also incontrovertibly indifferent to human fate. But certain groups formulate the "laws of nature" for specific purposes. Nature has been attributed with approved human values and ideals to validate and arise above, debate particular visions and ideologies.

Following the original Greek definition in all its catholicity, nature is deemed to be everything material that exists, then, strictly speaking, nothing can be unnatural. However, the distinction between the natural and the unnatural (or artificial) is invariably made and, while nature has no conceptual opposite, we usually think of it as human culture. Indeed, without a concept of culture

---

36. As quoted in Peter Coates, *Nature: Western Attitudes Since Ancient Times*, Berkeley: University of California Press, 1998, p. 3.

as the works of humankind, there can be no concept of nature. Some ancient Greek thinkers assumed that the original condition of mankind prior to social and political organization was a state of nature governed by natural laws. Depending on one's standpoint, humanity had either fallen from this state of grace, where it had been unencumbered by institutions, or had risen beyond its barbaric confines through the salutary mechanism of culture and human laws.

In Aristotle's *Physics*, a vital issue was the distinction between natural entities whose essence is innate — things that do what they do themselves — and artificial entities whose essence derives from an external source: the artist who sculpt a rock, the stone mason who builds a house. Hence, the difference between a marble cliff and a statue, a stone and a doorstep. Nineteenth-century American trans-cendentalist writer Ralph Waldo Emerson summarized this broad division of the world into the created and the creative (culture and man) on the one hand and the uncreated (nature) on the other:

> Nature, in the common sense, refers to the essences unchanged by man; space, the air, the river, the leaf. *Art* is applied to the mixture of his will with the same things, as in a house, a canal, a statue, a picture.

Emerson sought a further distinction, however, derived from German idealism, between "me" (spirit, soul, mind, and maker, i.e. ,consciousness) and "not me" (world, body, matter, the made, i.e. phenomena):

> Philosophically considered, the universe is composed of *Nature* and the *Soul*. Strictly speaking, therefore, all that is separate from us, all which philosophy distinguishes as the NOT ME, that is, both nature and art, all other men and my own body, must be ranked under this name, NATURE.[37]

The different meanings of nature discussed so far, with the exception of Emerson's, are all more or less predicated on nature's essentialism, the separation of nature and culture, and nature's superiority or inferiority to culture. But precisely which aspects of culture are most responsible for setting people apart from Nature? The answer for the ancient Greeks was reason. Early twentieth-century existentialist philosophy, by attributing supreme freedom and autonomy to the individual, posited the widest distance between people and nature.

Since the early modern analysis and interpretation of the relationship between humankind and nature presupposed the existence of all previous stages of thinking on this matter; Bacon, Descartes and Newton are best approached in terms of their collective impact. It is not primarily an account of their innovative ideas, or because they directly or indirectly inspired great masses of people, that I single out Bacon, Descartes and Newton for special attention. These luminaries feature here mainly in their capacity as spokesmen who articulated most effectively those areas of shared thought that sprang from the needs of particular groups.

---

37. As quoted in Peter Coates, *Nature: Western Attitudes Since Ancient Times*, p. 6.

Commentators over the past two decades have found no ambiguity in the beliefs or purpose of the man who inherited the Renaissance idea of mastery over nature through knowledge and expressed it with peerless aplomb. In the writings of Bacon (1561–1626), nature is forever being moulded, enslaved and penetrated. Goodies and secrets are wrested or coaxed from her. For Bacon, knowing nature was not an end in itself. His aphorism, "human knowledge and human power met in one" (usually abbreviated to "knowledge itself is power"), was no more rhetorical flourish. The goal of what Max Scheler in the 1920s dubbed *Herrschaft-Swissen* (knowledge for the sake of dominion) was manipulation and mastery. With Bacon, the question "what is nature?" Became inseparable from "what can we do with nature?"

What previous generations might have seen merely as harmless horticultural dabbling and ambitions; have been given a sinister spin by recent green commentators. Those who dwell on those aspects of Bacon's thought and writing that approach nature as a set of measurable, re-arrangeable, infinitely malleable components. They only recognized limits on interference with natural processes are those of human ingenuity and contrivance.

In most environmentalism, humans are viewed as protectors of the environments but not direct participants in ecosystem processes. There is a loophole in it, as it does not address the full range of ecological relationships between humans as a species and their environment. And such a loophole seriously undermines the prospect for a harmo-nious co-existence. Humans are part of nature and subject to the same broad principles as are other organisms.

Clearly, humans are in some ways different from other species, but there is no compelling reason for excluding them from nature.

Today, the environmentalist can only implore us to try to conceive of ourself and our purpose not in opposition to an environment, which is beginning to fight back, but through the surrounding world, which may support us forever if we learn to base our cultures upon ideals that allow the earth to flourish. It is the idea of nature independent of humanity which is fading, which needs to be replace by a nature that includes us, which we can only understand to the extend that we can find a home in the enveloping flow of forces which is only ever partially in our control. David Rothenberg said:

> there is no such thing as a pure wild nature, empty of human conception. The moment we identify it as such, it becomes ours! The minute we call some area of the earth separate from our influence, we are putting human constraints on the environment.[38]

Following the "modern divide" between man and nature, it made the doors open for further scientific investigation of nature. There are many implications of the scientific thesis as regards the concept of nature. One of the most important implications is the distinction between man and nature on the basis of rationality. Given this view that man is the only conscious being, environment becomes an

38. David Rothenberg, "The Green House from Down Deep: What can Philosophy do for Ecology," *Pan Ecology,* 7, no. 2 (Spring 1992) : 1-3.

object. Therefore, the environment must be exploited to the fullest for the benefit of man.

So, modern man after the Age of Reason does not have any respect for the environment. He does not realize that by destroying the environment, he destroys himself.

Nature supports and sustains us and we ought to protect it, but we are so increasingly concerned with our own little selves that we are out of touch with nature. Philosophers need to ask, in theory, whether nature is for real, to know, in practice, whether and how ethicists ought to conserve it. The less we really know about nature, the less we can or ought to save nature for what it is in itself, intrinsically. We cannot correctly value and preserve what we do not, to some degree, correctly know.

4

Critique of Preservation Schemes

THE earlier discussion refers to the time in the history of mankind, which is the glorious age of Science and Technology. Under the spell of such a world-view, man became obsessed and blinded by concepts like *development, modernization* and *progress*. As a result, he did not find it wrong to experiment, modify and destroy nature to better himself. His philosophy was; it is all right to destroy, modify and experiment with nature as long as it helps man to better his living. Under this scheme of understanding, exploitation and undue harnessing of nature was never questioned.

But this glorious age did not last long as it was doomed when man confronted the greatest threat from nature as a result of his own actions. Today, nature is seen revolting against man with all the terms like ozone-hole, green-house effect, global warming, acid rain and so on.

While recognizing the conflict between the "model of development" and long-term health of our planet, the United Nations organized the "Earth Summit" in Rio-de-Janeiro, Brazil during early June 1992. About 80 Heads of Nations and representatives of over 150 governments attended the conference. For the first time ever, the lifestyle of the affluent industrial societies was linked with the environmental danger to our planets earth.

The outcome of the conference was significant as, the importance of the environment in the local and regional politics came in focus. They realized that our planet is no longer the same, so there is an urgent message to drive home that our planet earth is in danger. From then onwards, environmental awareness programme is conducted all over the world, with a message to create awareness in all human beings that we have a role to play to preserve the enviro-nment as responsible people.

Even in India, the Non-Governmental Organizations (NGOs) have been able to pressurize the governments in a decisive manner. The power of "environmental activism" was visible in opposition to various projects like Narmada Sagar Project (NSP) in Madhya Pradesh and Sardar Sarovar Project (SSP) in Gujarat.

There was a time in the history of environmental movements when there was strong opposition and persistence by the peoples, especially by the tribal community against even the slightest intervention in the name of development. On investigation, it can be rightly said that such apprehensiveness and persistence were not just founded but something that stems out from the conviction and commitment these tribals had for the nature.

The tribal women of Advani village in Tehri-Garhwal had tied the sacred thread around trees, actually hugged the trees, faced police firing and later courted arrest. The movement was born in a small hilly village of the upper reaches of Himalayas in 1972 that became famous as the CHIPKO Movement (chipko means to embrace).

The movement basically aimed at saving trees on the Himalayan slopes from the axes of greedy contractors, but its objectives were broad-based. It questioned the development based on the ruthless butchery of nature to achieve "short-term" gains. It challenged the belief that forests mean only timber and emphasized their role in making soil, water and pure air, which are the basis of life. These villagers believed that every standing green tree in the forest is sentry to protect us from avalanches and landslides to save our soils and conserve our water. It was this philosophy, which popularized this movement.

Bishnoi movement is also another of this kind. According to the history of Bishnoi, in AD 1737 an official of Jodhpur State started felling of Khejri trees in Khejerli village for burning of lime needed for the state. This was opposed by the Bishnois of the village, because like the most tribals they also believed that all living things including the animals and trees have a right to survive and share all resources. The initiative in this case was taken by a woman. Amritadevi, a mother of three minor daughters, who was the first to sacrifice her life by hugging the tree that was being axed. She defied the orders of the state and tried to prevent the felling of the Khejri tree. She was killed for opposing to cut the tree. Her example was followed first by her three daughters and later on by a long chain of Bishnoi men, women and children. For every tree felled in Khejerli village, a man, woman and child made an extreme sacrifice. In all 363 Bishnois from Khejerli and adjoining villages sacrificed their lives. When this news reached the Maharaja of Jodhpur, he apologized for the mistake committed. He ordered a royal decree prohibiting cutting of trees and hunting of animals in all Bishnoi village and also ordered a severe penalty to those violating the order.

Bishnois noticed the interdependence of plants, birds and animals, and understood their role in sustaining the quality of life in the arid Thar Desert. They not only understood it themselves but also had the wisdom of influencing generation of people to preserve it by weaving it with their action. And, this makes the Bishnois stand apart from countless other communities in India and in the world, in generating environmental awareness through the sacrifice they made in preserving the environment.

In the above discussions, the desire and concern to preserve the nature is from within. The tribals in these two instances deliberately opposed to destruction of nature, motivated and disciplined by their tradition. Here the resistance and opposition were only against the external incursions. It was an opposition to something, which was not really in their way of life. Their desire to have a close communion with nature was *pure* and *straight*. This kind of preservation idea about nature stands in contrast with the modern man's interest to preserve nature. For the Bishnois, when they wanted to protect and preserve those trees — it was not because they were afraid of the impending survival dangers due to the destruction of nature like modern man is. Such a desire to protect the trees was not a new thing, but something already embedded in them and in their tradition.

On the other hand, the modern man's desires and urge to protect and preserve nature is altogether a new phenomenon. It is a recent phenomenon as a result of the realization that they are exposed to danger due to their merciless raping of nature. Here the desire to preserve nature is an imposed one.

Of course, the modern tribal is no different in their exploitation of nature from others. He fails to realize that the growth of all civilization whether traditional or modern depends primarily upon the materials of nature. As such, instead of citing living and practical examples by respecting and practising their age-long value loaded tradition they themselves become the *exploiters* and the *exploited*. Lured by the terms like *development*, *modernization* and *progress*, they also start looking at nature only with a desire to benefit from it. Even in Ao villages (Nagaland), the same pheno-menon has set in. Timber contractors carried off much of the jungles, poachers killed the last wild bear to supply its skins and pluck the orchids for the sake of money.

During one of my trips, I met an impressive elderly man living in Ao village — a real tribesman: who claims to possess the tiger power (a tiger-man). This idea of tiger-man is at the core of Ao tradition, whose role in their tribal society is, much more than a modern ecologist or a biologist, because of his amazing in-depth knowledge and under-standing about the working of nature. He tried to teach his family and others; but they are not interested, he laments.

As for modern development programmes, let me cite here an example. There are no proper roads to *Watiyim* village in the Ao area of Nagaland. But the villagers do not mind. "Some years ago, a road was constructed but it was meant for the timber contractors. And, in a few years, the forest vanished," says Tali, an elderly villager, who himself showed a deep concern to regenerate the forest. "We need forest, not roads," he adds.

The village's rich forest was cleared when it was given on lease to timber merchants. Now, they are left with nothing. The damage and the shortage are so severe in some areas that they have difficulty even to search for firewood. Due to such activities, tribals are feeling the pressure of widespread deforestation that is being carried out to feed the flourishing timber industry. And, it is obvious that a vast treasure house of ethno-botanical knowledge will be lost if this trend is not reversed.

Now the question is — whose benefit at who's lost? Development in what sense? Is it destruction at the cost of development?

I may be permitted briefly to touch on two important words that are central to this debate — *Development* and *growth*. The original concept and meaning of development implied "an unfolding from within." In another words, "to draw out the latent and inherent potential of the people, and their systems to tackle their own problems." This essential continuing creative exercise in itself, stands in sharp contrast, to what is today, described as *development* — the superimposition of an external reality onto the lifestyles of the indigenous people. Similarly, when we talk of *growth*, it has to be with balance and harmony as it occurs in nature. Societal growth has to confirm to the natural orders — anything beyond that would be a calamity.

When we have people living in the forest and the forest is threatened in the name of development, the life systems of the people are also threatened. Also if a big project like a dam is built, then the people are displaced and they are forced to migrate. If they do that they are waging a greater war in the name of development, i.e., not only destroying the natural environment but also the life of the people. Because development cannot be at the expense of natural environment or destroying something.

Having said this let me also make it most explicit and clear that my intention is not to descend to an emotional tirade, for or against, the present model of development. I am also not against technology, modernity, but plead for a rational unbiased holistic philosophical debate on such issues.

Failed and dissatisfied with the unqualified and random modern development schemes, there's a great deal of talk and action these days, of *sustainable development*. Sustainable development means development that meets the needs of the present without compromising the ability of the future generations to meet their own needs. In other words, sustainable development stands for a concept that reconciles the improvement of man's economic and social living conditions with long-term security of the natural basis in life. This means that protection of the environment must not be at the end of the list, but must be an integral part of all development. As such, sustainable development requires ecological as well as economic and socio-cultural factors to be taken into account, both in national and global context. In the task of implementing this development concept all countries bear a common but differentiated responsibility. For this reason, the industrialized countries in particular are called upon to cut their consumption of resources and to reduce environmental burden by means of rigorous national precautionary policies.

In an attempt to achieve environmentally-friendly logging, *Mil Madeireira*, a Brazil-based forestry company, has evolved a way to cut trees in such a way that when a tree is cut, it falls in an area where few other trees would be affected. The company's logging method has been acknowledged by conservationists in their fight to stop the devastation of the world's largest tropical rain forest.

Recently, Hardwood buyers and sellers gathered in Brazil's Amazon capital Manaus to seek ways to preserve the nation's vast rainforests. And, one of the aims of "The First Workshop of Sustainable Forest Production in the Amazon" was to show loggers in the region how to map, select, cut, and transport their tropical hardwood with the least possible damage to the forest. These logging practices used by *Mil Madeireira* is said to cost some 30 per cent more than the traditional methods, but the company says the final bill can be reduced by wasting less wood and stresses that the result is to heal the surrounding trees. "It is all in the planning,"[1] a spokesperson for *Mil* told fellow Amazon loggers.

Keeping the maxim "Environment with Development," there is much debate about concepts like "environmentally sound" and "appropriate technology" today. The idea is that, the technologies must be chosen

1. *Down to Earth* (15 November 1999) : 40.

by taking into account environment, economic and social goals. Under this sustainable development, the relationship between environment and development is seen as inevitable, intimate and inseparable. The argument is that, if concerns are restricted purely to developmental objectives, and the environmental context of the society is disregarded, then the consequential deterioration of the habitat leads to an indirect, but nevertheless serious, frustration of those very objectives. Because, if environmental considerations are ignored, development cannot be sustained in the long run and developmental goals are imperilled.

This view (the restated development objectives) of development is seen as fundamentally different from one in which development is equated with *growth*. It is claimed to be principally concerned with the quality of life and the environment, rather than only on goods and services. When asked about how environment has to be taken care of even after welcoming industries, Ajit Jogi said,

> sustainable development is the key. We are conscious of the ecological and environmental needs. At the same time, we cannot keep the tribal people out of mainstream development. There has to be a lot of growth in the industrial sector, but it has to be sustainable.[2]

Scientists nowadays are found engaged in developing some kind of eco-friendly technologies or the other.

---

2. Ajit Jogi, the first Chief Minister of Chattisgarh, speaks to *Down to Earth* on sustainable development of the new State. *Down to Earth* (15 January 2001) : 37.

Researchers in Israel are said to have developed a rechargeable battery based on magnesium that could provide a viable alternative to the other technologies. Back home even in India the first Indian eco-friendly refrigerator is reported to have been manufactured. Godrej Appliances Limited (GAL) has begun producing India's first refrigerator that uses hydrocarbon (HCs). The company carried out research for four years in co-ordination with the Ministry of Environment and Forests and two companies based in Switzerland and Germany before launching their new product on January 22, 2000.[3]

With the idea of sustainable development being pushed to the front, world has stepped into the *era of sustainable business development* also called the *age of eco-design*. Eco design is all about redesigning of products while taking environmental aspects into consideration and simultaneously balancing the economic as well as ecological requirements of the product. It means better products, less waste, more efficiency, and reduction in pollution and use of raw material. *Bamboo Boards and Beyond*: exhibition of bamboo furniture by the National Institute of Design, Ahmedabad which was on view from January 22 to January 26, 2001 is one such example. The exhibition showcased how bamboo, a cheaper and sustainable alternative to wood, can be used for making furniture with the same kind of finish as wood. The question, however, is whether bamboo could really emerge as an alternative material. "Of course," says M.P. Rajan, faculty member of industrial design, NID and the project head of Bamboo

3. *Down to Earth* (15 March 2001) : 47.

Boards and Beyond. "We are looking at bamboo as a fully sustainable, eco-friendly industrial material of the future."[4]

In deeper consideration, this remarkably slippery concept of "sustainable development" seems to add to conventional ideas of development with the goal of a harmonious and unified management capacity, to ensure that exploitation of "nature" is alright as long as it brings development to man. There is little effort to understand and modify the development process itself, in a manner that will bring it into greater harmony with the needs of the people and with the need to maintain balance in the environment. The biggest challenge for humanity is: How to get more from our natural resources even without destroying them.

In order to curb the problems brought about by the modern mantra of *development* and *progress* either of sustainable or of unsustainable kind, similar double-edged alternatives like "forestation programme" has come. This forestation programme also, despite its promising ideals and goals, seems without much help. Instead, many criticize it. And one of the many reasons is that, such a programme is mostly economic based and not solely to regenerate the forest for posterity. As such, today even the villagers are sceptical about the programme. Many feel, that such agencies come with a view to plant trees, but they are more interested in exploring the forest and collecting plant species for their own use.

---

4. *Down to Earth* (28 February 2001) : 54.

In sharp contrast to this is the traditional tribal practice of protecting forest. For them, forest protection is not an economic activity; it is a social, and more of religious value. "We don't harm a tree, even if it is dead," says Pangerchiba, a villager. It's not that they are too dumb to spoil the place and the trees, but it's because they don't want to. Unlike the modernist, even today, almost every village, where there is a community protecting the forests, is a success story.

"No conservation strategy will succeed in India unless the biomass requirement of the local communities are harmoniously integrated into the strategy. The present conservation has an in-built dimension that alienates local people,"[5] said B.J. Krishnan. But, this is more easily said than done. Whether it is the Keoladeo Ghana National Park in Bharatpur, Rajasthan, or the Namdapha National Park in Arunachal Pradesh, most of these communities are under tremendous pressure to give up their traditional way of living.

A prime example of the lack of science in wildlife management affecting a local community is from the Keoladeo Ghana National Park. Following a ban on grazing buffaloes in the marshes of Bharatpur in 1982, a bloody conflict ensued between the forest department and the local grazers, resulting in a shoot-out that claimed seven human lives. Later some of the buffaloes came back to save the Park. A villager said,

---

5. B. J. Krishnan Advocate and Founder of the *Save Nilgiris Campaign*, Quoted in *Down to Earth* (15 March 2000) : 35.

> Scientists recommended a ban on grazing. We listened to them. Ten years later, they say grazing is good. We cannot listen to them all the time when their research gives contradictory results.

A similar story is from the Namdapha National Park in Miao, Changlang district of Arunachal Pradesh, which is the 15th Tiger Reserve of India and was declared as such in 1983. Prior to the existence of this National Park in this area, the wilderness was the main source of livelihood for the eco people like the Lisu — a small community who lives in the fringes of this park touching the Indo-Burma border. The declaration of this area as the National Park sounded an achievement to the worldwide populace especially for India. However, from the point of view of the locals the park is nothing but a cruel freedom curtailment. The declaration of the place as a protected area, it means that no trespasses are allowed. It is difficult since no other means of surface communication exists. Restriction in cutting firewood and collecting wild edible plants means an attack on the very life of the people. Unexposed group of people like the Lisus would not be able to understand and perceive the environmental strategies meant for the welfare of all.

During a visit to the Park for a National Seminar on "Biodiversity And Indigenous Knowledge" organized by North East Biodiversity Research Cell, NEHU, Shillong in 2001, a villager said, "we do not want a park here, villagers are cheated in the name of conservation. We do not want any conservation." When asked about how they find the park, many villagers those who reside near and around the park expressed the wish to recover their forest. The tensions and hatred among the people for the terms "environment" and "conservation" is very obvious.

In the light of all these, the talk about Environment Conservation Programme seems to have less significance today. And the examples discussed above are ample evidence to show that they do not basically cater to the actual needs and environments of the people, they are domains of influence and affluence of national or multinational elites and powers.

Modern man in their desperate attempts to salvage from the menace of nature express himself absurdly many a time. After destroying nature, now they are interested in teaching the tribals (in fact, whose insight into the working of nature is a spectacle) about environment preservation. Such kinds of calls appear absurd and meaningless. Along with their mantra of forestation programme, the practices of shifting cultivation system of the tribals in the hilly areas are questioned. Alternatives are given, but I feel the whole problem doesn't end here. As it involves practical — survival issues. It appears that the modern man is confused and I think they should not try to confuse the tribals in the villages by infusing bits and pieces of their own confusion. Such a view merits a close philosophical analysis.

Modern technological man, intoxicated by highly advanced technology and materialistic viewpoints, has changed the environment for his vested interests to such an extent that even his very existence is threatened. Disillusioned with his own creation; he tried to make amends by destroying almost everything from the plastics bags in India to the Mega-dams in the US.

While environmentalist and the governments are on a warpath over dams in India, construction workers in the US began dismantling them. To save the salmon from extinction, the US government is at present imposing curbs on the construction of dams. Further, the US-based Federal Energy Regulatory Commission (FERC) is demanding that fish ladders (special dam structures to facilitate the migratory path of fish) be built into the existing dams if their licenses are to be renewed. That is often so expensive that companies usually opt to destroy the dam instead. In a more drastic step, dams obstructing the migratory path of the salmon are being razed to allow the fish free passage. It is said, that at least 100 dams have been removed from waterways in the US; another 100 are either committed or are under active consideration for removal. According to Chris Zimmer of the US-based environmental organization *Save Our Wild Salmon*, "populations of wild life, such as bear, eagle, mink and river otter, for whom the salmon is a source of food, drops drastically," he says, adding: "Besides the dangers posed to wildlife, the north-west forests in the US are partly built on the nutrients salmon bring back from the sea."[6] Wild salmons are considered the energy fuels of the environment. So, every individual salmon is important and when a river is dammed, their very existence is threatened.

Constructions of dams were the *mantra* of the 1950s. With the emphasis shifting to restoration of degraded

---

6. *Down to Earth* (15 November 1999) : 30.

aquatic environment, the "1990s saw a drastic reversal. Nations began to contemplate letting the rivers run free again. Why? The social, economic and environmental costs far exceeded the benefits. Ironically, the US — which had over the past 100 years championed the cause of dam building — is now ordering their destruction. Today, they view dams as the biggest menace to river ecology, wildlife, aquatic habitat of fish and ultimately humans.

Newton's third law states: "every actions has equal and opposite reaction." This will equally apply to man's relationship with nature as it relates to application of force and nature. There was a time, the modern man claimed to have conquered nature but nature is silent in its persistent influence over man. Now the situation is such that the nature is revolting against man and thereafter conquering him in every aspect.

The irony of the US dam dismantling move is a clear indication of how the environment influences the man. And, this is a significant shift in the history of environment movement. First they constructed the dams not only at the cost of riverine ecosystems but also threatened the very survival of both human beings and the wildlife. And, today, the same technological man is all geared up to dismantle these dams in order to restore the riverine ecosystem. Here, we see a role reversal. Humans tried to modify and influence nature but environment soon influenced them in shaping their thoughts and actions. Everything has reversed.

With biodiversity concerns being pushed upfront in recent times, in the context of global change, scientific validation of *traditional ecological knowledge* (TEK) has assumed greater significance. Environmentalists looking for alternative ways have started to look into tribal eco-philosophy. In other words, traditional knowledge has been lauded as an alternative to collective wisdom relevant to a variety of matters at a time when existing norms, values and laws are increasingly called into question. As a result, many agencies and projects enter the tribal areas with varied environmental proposals. Some come with the idea to protect the rare flora and fauna, wild animals, while, some with a proposal about forestation programme.

Modern scientific approaches are in themselves insufficient to address today's complex environmental problems. They attempt to isolate a problem, while the traditional approach examines problems in their totality.

The traditional knowledge of indigenous communities, which was for a long time viewed with skepticism by the world has now, acknowledged its importance. Thinking along the line, Kiran Karnik said, "Environment to me is the way tribal communities look at it constantly interacting with it and respecting it."[7] Emphasizing the importance to learn from the eco-centric world-view of the tribals, B.K. Agrawal had to say:

> It is from the tribals that we learn and celebrate life. I'm trying to learn from the tribals and not trying to teach them. As a modern man, I suddenly find that the two institutions that give stability to modernity are collapsing: the state and the market. I suddenly find myself irrelevant. In this situation,

---

7. Kiran Karnik, on "ways to popularize environment issues," *Down to Earth* (15 April 2001) : 50.

> I am searching for alternate ways of being and am finding in the tribal way such an alternative. [8]

The *Tsürangkong* people in the Ao area of Nagaland, are renowned for their unique system of fish cum paddy rice cultivation. (Of course, nowadays experts are also widely involved in this activity.) People visiting their beautiful land are regaled with tales of this agriculture, and much else, as examples of *ancient folkways*. On a research field trip to this place in 2001, I was fascinated to learn, that it was, in fact, a recent creation. I offer this instance of how fish came to paddy, as an example of sound and keen traditional tribal knowledge about nature.

As narrated by the villagers, the fish-cum-paddy system evolved gradually in the 1950s and 1960s. Many government environmental and agricultural extension agents urged the villagers to start fishponds. Several farmers experimented, without much success. It seems that it was the villagers there who first suggested that it did not make sense to build new ponds in the midst of already existing terraced paddies. However, when they faced innumerable problems, they tried one small invention after another. First, the fingerlings ate up the young rice plants. Gradually, after experimentation, the villagers figured out how to introduce the fingerlings at a time when the rice plants were strong enough to withstand their gnawing. It took years of experimentation to find the right plants and small creatures to introduce into the paddies, in the right amounts and mixtures — to provide food for the fish

---

8. Prof. B.K. Agrawal, *Commenting about Tribal worldview in a National Seminar on "Rationality And Tribal Thought: An Indian Perspective,"* North Eastern Hill University, Shillong, 2001.

without harming the rice — all with a constant exchange of wisdom and mutual concern between the tribesman and nature.

This really is an inspiring example, as set by the *Tsürangkonger*. If such wisdom had been duplicated around the world in the 1950s and 1960s, we might now be living in a much healthier environment.

Today, realizing the value of such centuries old indigenous knowledge, development is now "Back to Basics." There is a great deal of talk about *community-based* development programmes. The idea is to integrate indigenous knowledge in joint forest and developmental projects. This is considered and taken into account by many environmentalists as a better option. One such example is the varied community-based environment management and Development programme undertaking by the CIDA sponsored project "Nagaland Empowerment of People through Economic Development" (NEPED) in Nagaland. An official involved in the programme had this to say, "We have so much to learn from them. We came to teach them but we end up learning from them instead. Their insight into the working of nature is just unbelievable!"

In spite of saying all these, we have few models for expert/community partnership that truly nurture the desired goals. The story of how drought prone communities of Bhaonta Kolyala village in the Alwar district of Rajasthan, had rejuvenated their traditional water harvesting systems is one such example.[9]

9. *Down to Earth,* (30 April 2000) : 24-31.

Then again the revival of river Arvari is the result of people's participation at the village levels at water conservation, employing traditional practices. Momentum to the efforts was provided by Tarun Bharat Sangh (TBS), a Non-Governmental Organization (NGO) working in the area, which since 1985 had mobilized the people at every village in the district to conserve water. *Johads* are crescent-shaped mud dams for the collection of water between two hills. These water harvesting structures were much in use until some 200-400 years when the hills around the area were green and full of wildlife. TBS had advocated the people to repair old *johads* and to make new ones. These, built in the watershed of the river Arvari, were an effort to catch the sparse rain that falls in the region. The *johads* were aimed at recharging ground water levels, but these check dams not only enhanced the water table, it made the seasonal rivulet flow perennially. Arvari has been flowing continually since 1995. With the water bodies recharged, the once arid lands now can grow two crops. Now the villagers have once again reminded themselves that everything in the area is related to the river and they do not want to forfeit it again.

But even in areas where such indigenous knowledge is taken into consideration, some say that it is insufficient. "We are just taking the knowledge and trying to integrate it not knowing what it means for the people concerned,"[10] says Klaus Seeland. The government agencies or NGOs who conduct different ventures in tribal habitats should

---

10. Klaus Seeland is the Chairperson, Forest Policy and Forest Economics, Swiss Federal Institute of Technology, *Down to Earth* (30 April 2001) : 18-19.

take social, ecological and religious aspects also into consider-ation. He further adds, "one should have a clear concept of tribal knowledge when we integrate it in activities like joint forest management."

The question is who should plead for whose involvement? Calling for the indigenous people's involve-ment seems absurd. And, I think it makes not much sense trying to manage the tribal environments; don't we do so in towns and cities, which contribute the greatest threat to environment? Is it just another way of discrimination. Tribal land was destroyed because of the modern man's interven-tion and if they just withdraw their activities, they'll have not much problem. The modern man needs to be involved with the tribals in loving and caring for the environment.

Again one is sceptical about the idea that the modern man learn from the tribal. It is sceptical in the sense that they might learn only to make their programme successful and ultimately to salvage themselves. As there is possibility of learning only for a purpose, i.e., to integrate it in their programme, but not really learn to love and live harmoniously with nature as tribal do.

The philosophical question one must ask here is — what are the reasons that encourage community-based develop-ment? As pointed out; too often, such schemes come in with a *blueprint* — a fixed plan for progress. Again and again, we have seen such approaches introduce alien factors that take over and destabilize local culture and ecosystems like an invasive weed. When this happens there's an imbalance between the innovation and the local context. And, I think, today the fate of humanity hinges on the claim, a necessarily political one, that human life requires a life-world facilita-ting the ability to weave levels and facets of reality into holistic coherence, such that the earth recovers its generative status as *place,* not merely economic *space.*

One needs to look closely at this, because it is the point where culture meets agriculture, traditional ways meet modern ways, global meets local. What is it that makes something *traditional* rather than *modern*? Again, the dialectic of thing and context is all-important. To bring something within traditional ways is to establish dialectic of thing and context.

Today, there's much talk about the traditional tribal knowledge, but have we thought deeply enough about how much we would have to change if we were to work hand in hand between traditional and modern knowledge or between local and expert knowledge? Scholars have argued in the recent writing, that such partnerships are necessary to build the ecological citizenship needed to combat environmental challenges. Why are such partnerships necessary? Scholars argue that they can combat the underlying causes of the environmental crisis and social inequalities that are increasing globally. The term *partnership* is misleading. In many ways, it is better to think of it as a process of de-localization, in which tribal people become the victims. To what extent are philosophers, complicit in this? In recent writings, we have argued that, for over 100 years, academic systems of research and teaching have been key factors in propagating *technocratic managerialism* a way of thinking that sees the world as a machine that can be controlled by instrumentally rational thought that is put under the control of guilds of elite, educated experts.

Efforts to blend the place rooted knowledge of the tribesman and the technical or modern knowledge of academics are seldom harmonious or tension-free. Differences grounded in history, culture and class; require thoughtful recognition and negotiation by all concerned with such efforts. Challenge lies in the mutual generation of a new, practically relevant rhetoric of co-operative knowledge and action for the groups involved. Here the philosophers trained in unbiased rational discourse and steeped in traditional and tribal cultures can have a very effective role.

Undoubtedly all heartfelt calls, from many and diverse quarters, for new forms of community, academic partnership, and a revolving of tribal eco-world-view, can be seen as an important and sincere effort to combat technocratic managerialism and its ecological and political abuses. But, what is tribal world-view? Too often, tribal world-view is thought of as the thought and action of uneducated people. I would argue that tribal world-view is better thought of as thinking that is *placed* — that is at least potentially rooted in cosmogenic agency. It is thought that is rooted in particular lives, grounded in actually existing locales and histories. It is thought that is deeply existential thought that cannot escape givenness, from the unfolding pressure of time itself as it is inevitably experienced within personal and collective narratives.

Our culture, determines our attitude towards our relation to things around us. As Rabindranath Tagore once said:

> The soil in which we are born is the soil of our village, the mother earth in whose lap we receive our nourishment from day to-day-our educated elite abstracted from the primal basis wander about in high heaven of ideas like aimless clouds removal from this our home.

Though Tagore was not talking about the biodiversity conservation he was displeased with the discarding of the traditional practices, for to him all traditional things are important ingredients of life.

Modern man endowed with reason, is said to work on nature to suit his own purpose. Science and technology, on the other, as the product and expression of reason, are said to liberate man from the bond of nature: the more we know of the laws of nature, the better we are said to be equipped for exploiting her and making her subservient to our human goals and comforts. It is indubitable that in nature man is a distinctive being by virtue of his power of abstract thinking. Given such an interpretation — Where has this outlook led us? The answer is: An ever-increasing degradation of our environment.

It can be said legitimately that the Age of Reason has failed us. It seems to be just an age of narrow and scientific reason, but it has not really brought about the age of wisdom. Such an age is said to have failed, because despite the many global attempts to preserve the environment, the ecological crisis is still on its march. Our modern culture in crisis has reacted by rejecting total tradition and its ecological sense. The remedy has been worse than the problem itself, since the superstructure is made to rest on a vacuum.

I wish to conclude that the environmental crisis that beleaguers us stems from a world-view crisis, a crisis that the modern environmentalist generally ignores. Still further, that the resolution of this world-view crisis can only be achieved by reformulating thoughts along rational lines, insured with an environmental philosophy and sensibility.

All the sophisticated social organization, science and technology will not work unless we change our world-view. Because, whatever idea of nature, science generates, it is man's own science, his own construction, his own judgement of the world, and the interpretations, self-made, of his own experience (the scientific world-view). Unless the idea of humanity being part of nature is fully elaborated, it will remain vague, a mere platitude. Also the idea that nature is the sole reality, the main foundation of a naturalistic philosophy, needs clarification and greater enunciation.

While the entire debate of modernity centres around the underlying dualism of man and nature, which the debates appear unable to destroy. For the tribals, to whose view I will shortly turn, their relation with nature is one of *communion*.

As such the modern man is seen here in need to renew their perspective of the earth and its essential and existential connection to life in general and to human life in particular, which the tribesman seems to radiate. Such a perspective would offer to the modern man a culture that emphasizes a holistic vision where Nature, Man and God make up a cosmotheandric integrated reality, where humans form an integral part of the wholeness of being.

While the theoreticians and the ethicists are busy fighting trying to supersede each other's theories, the preservationist and the environmentalists on the other hand, are busy trying to find the best plan and programme to preserve the environment. And, at the backdrop of this muddle to salvage the environment, I will try to see in the Ao world-view how they have lived with and preserved the environment without any tension since time immemorial in the next chapter.

5

The Ao Vision of Nature Preservation

THE mother earth as central to the organic cosmology as viewed by the tribals of north-eastern India was undermined by the scientific revolution, which labelled their view as "primitive" and crude forms of "tribalism." The rise of materialistic culture almost denuded the natural attire of the sacred mother earth and turned her into a dumping ground for industrial waste.

The ecological sensitivity, however, has rekindled interest in the values and concepts associated as an integral part of the pre-modern organic world-views. In this chapter I will limit myself to a discussion of the beliefs of the Aos of Nagaland.

The Aos are the tribal people who live in the Mokokchung district of the state of Nagaland. The etymology of the word, Ao, according to local tradition, meaning, went (i.e., went across the Dikhu river), a boundary river that divided Ao from Sangtam and Phom tribes. Those who came were called Aos, and those stayed back were called Mirirs, which consists of Sangtams,

Phoms, Changs and Konyaks.[1] The Aos are divided into six administrative ranges; Ongpangkong, Asetkong, Langpangkong, Changkikong, Japukong and recently, Tsürangkong. They got their local names according to different places but they are one and the same tribe known as the Aos who follow the patriarchal system, where the father is the head of the *Kibong* or family.

According to them the world including man is a sacred milieu in-dwelt by the spirit, thus no one species could conceivably assume that the whole existed for its benefits alone. Aos worship the Supreme Being as well as the rest of creation by addressing prayers to them. Prayers call upon the soil, forests and rivers to be gentle and to provide them abundantly. Here is an invocation of an Ao elder to the mother earth:

> Oh! Earth, when my people dig,
> Be kind to them
> Be fertile when they come to you with seeds
> And let the crops be healthy
> Do away any kind of impending disaster in the village
> Let there be a plentiful harvest.

The prayer is addressed to the mother earth, the forests and rivers, as they believed these are intelligent entities. The Aos personify nature in order to be able to communicate with them, and solicit their help for their own welfare. Here, an existing ecological sensitivity captures the spirit behind

1. Panger Imchen, Ancient Ao-Naga Religion and Culture, New Delhi: Har-Anand Publications, 1983, p. 20.

the enchantment of the world and sees everything existing in God and God in everything. There is a growing awareness of the presence of God in the world and the presence of the world including man in God.

As it is found in many tribal groups, Aos also do not have a scripture or creed that provides a systematic exposition about their world-view. Their religious ethos are embedded in myths, oral history and rituals. Unlike the other world-views, which teaches high anthropocentricism, the Aos have a different view of the world based on the co-creature-liness of all beings.

According to Ao religion, Lizaba the creator God or the Supreme Being has two connotations: Li means "Soil," and Jaba or Zaba means, "enter;" meaning "the one who enters the soil." Every year, the Aos observe a three days ritual called Lizaba Mong during the Ao sowing season (i.e., in the Month of March-April). On this day, Lizaba is believed to have entered the soil with the seeds and rises again along with the crops. So, such a belief makes them perceive the whole of creation as the manifestation of the Supreme Being. People experience the presence of the Supreme Being in the wind, the sun, the trees, and the rivers. This explains why they see the dynamic presence of the Supreme Being in creation.

On the days of Lizaba Mong, for three days and nights nobody can dig or plough the soil. People are not allowed even to fetch water or to collect firewood. In that way, Aos treat the soil with all kindness, concern and the utmost care. During these days, any actions or activities that may hurt the soil are discouraged rigorously.

The high reverence the Aos have for mother earth can be understood through an Ao myth. The myth says that a human, a tiger and God lived happily as one family with their mother . . . after the mother's death the three brothers decided to go separate ways. The loss of the mother brought chaos and separation. Without mother earth there is no unity between humans, animals and the Supreme Being. In other words, mother earth is the basis of life and unity of all. Thus, the earth/soil, for the tribals, is a material symbol through which people become one not only with the Supreme Being, but also with their ancestors, the spirits and the rest of creation.

Following from this belief the Aos consider the land as sacred. Before a person speaks in public, he will first drive his spear firmly into the ground where he stands and then only he can start his speech. It is a sign of swearing in the name of the soil that whatever he says is true and if he says anything, which is not true, he will be responsible for whatever the consequences.

The Aos in the past went to war when there was the case of land encroachment. They gave their lives for the sake of their land. They are staunch protectors of their land. They believe that without land they are not people. Every patch of forest, every mountain, and rock has a legend and a tale to tell. To part an inch of land is equivalent to giving away a portion of the self. Such a reverence or the belief keeps the balance between humans and nature. It holds life in balance and in harmony, which makes possible the preservation of nature, a reality.

Tribals view themselves as an integral component of the eco-system; this integrative viewpoint is equally obvious in every aspect of their life. Nature and its constituents have been traditionally preserved through an elaborate code of conduct considered to be in harmony with biological cycles, astral movements, climatic phenomena and the sacred geography of the land. They have amassed a whole lot of empirical knowledge on the basis of their experience whilst dealing with nature and natural resources. Such wisdom is based on the intrinsic realization that man and nature form part of an indivisible whole, and therefore should live in partnership with each other. One instance of such knowledge is: It is so believed by the Aos that, if the new moon appears to be red it indicates rainfall. In short, they live according to the direction of nature.

The guiding principles for preserving nature are embedded in the codified and often non-codified life practices that have evolved over centuries. These practices were intended to boost both social solidarity and for promoting environmental consciousness *per se*. Sometimes their preservation values are less explicit than social solidarity and religious norms; but that does not mean their preservation value is incidental. To supplement this idea here is an instance: The Ao elders usually admonished the youngsters by saying:

> *Akijangmenko liba sungdongla küokü tesük, tsükbala semchasemnur teshi tenarong jak pekoru*

Which means trees in the nearby surrounding should not be cut-off for firewood; and, if you burn such firewood you and your generation will become deaf. Interestingly, it indirectly presupposes a preservation ethic. It speaks about the desire of a balanced communion with nature. They are told not to cut trees where the forest is already disturbed by human habitations, hence man is advised to go to the deep forest to meet their needs, where nature is still bountiful enough to survive the intervention.

It is interesting to note here that human welfare, as well as socio-economic values are not ruled out whereas, the welfare of "nature" is taken care of. The tribesman's belief therefore, warrants an integral approach to natural resource management subsuming cultural, economic and ecological principles, to redress preservational issues in a more holistic way.

The traditional world vision of Ao, presents us with a philosophy of ecological harmony, where harmony is achieved by the collaborative endeavours of interrelated parts. All entities entail each other, where each one needs the other for being what it is; one does not transcend the other. Here, harmony is achieved in an interdependent, collaborative and responsible milieu. Environment or the rest of the creation is not an "other" but an immediate dimension of ourselves. Let me refer here to the Ao tale of how the rat brought and gave rice to man.

When the Aos were in Chungliyimti,[2] they did not know what rice was. One day, a rat said to man: "I will present you something if you promise to give me a decent funeral when I die." The man agreed and subsequently, the rat presented him of the rice and also showed him how good it

---

2. The tradition says that the Ao originated out of stones near this city Chungliyimti.

was to eat. After few days, the rat decided to test the man's good faith. One day the rat pretended to be dead. But, instead of fulfilling his promise the man after seeing the dead rat said: "What a dead rat, poke a stick under it and throw it in the river." The rat, which was not really dead, was angered and said: "As you have broken the promise, from today, I will always eat your rice before you and will defecate."

The myth explains that if we misuse the rest of creation, it will turn against us. Humans failed to keep their promise to the rat and as a result the harmony is disturbed. Here, the man is seen as the source of his own problems.

For a tribesman, nature is alive, and its powers are distinguished as personal because human-self directly experiences them. Humans live in the realm of a throbbing, personal nature, the domain of sacred entities. Therefore, human's position *vis-à-vis* the world is not one of exploitation but of co-existence. The idea expressed in their myth and songs is a clear indication of a fantastic teaching-learning process between man and the rest of creation. Take for instance the Ao song of "How the tree taught man to sing." One day when singing was not known by the Aos, a Chungliyimti girl was taking a bath at a riverbank. As she bathed, she kept saying — I've taken a bath I've taken a bath, to her utter surprise, the tree standing near the riverbank spoke and taught her to sing like this:

> I've taken a bath
> Damsel, the one who looks appealing
> The girl from Chungliyimti in her bodice
> Your tattooed legs brighten the way?
> As like the movement of the water.

Such close communion and reverential attitude towards the rest of creation is seen concretized in the various art forms, which constitute a way of transmitting the timeless truths of man-nature ethics. The Aos regarded an Ao warrior as a tiger for like him he protects his community from enemies. Aos decorate their traditional men's shawl *tsungkotepsu* with the picture of a tiger. The same kind of philosophy is also conveyed through the picture of a tiger seen encarved in most Ao village gates.

Ao religion, like any other tribal religion also does not have a founder or a reformer. In other words, their religion is not centred in any great historical person or persons. Rather, it is a religion centred on earth; the creation. Here, creation itself is the Supreme Being.

The Supreme Being appears in every being, tree, rock, flowers, beckons in every relationship and bursts forth in every ecosystem. What I wish to point out is that the Aos concept of nature cannot be understood without referring to religion. And, in the same way, one cannot understand their religion without referring to their account of creation. The love and wisdom of the Supreme Being are mediated through examining meticulously the objects around them. Thus, their whole religious system is embedded within the world of nature.

The Supreme Being is both within and beyond creation. He is personally involved within and outside creation. The Supreme Being is thus simultaneously transcendent and immanent. However, their myths and beliefs do not presuppose the Supreme Being to be everything and everything to be the Supreme Being. He is rather seen as manifested in natural objects. That is why the Aos can turn to the Supreme Being at every time and at any place.

In the Ao tradition, rituals are performed not only for social approval but also for Supreme Being's approval. For instance, before clearing the new jungle or cutting down the trees for cultivation, the village elders perform the "appropriate" rituals to gain the Supreme Being's approval. As the Aos pay great respect and reverence to trees, sometimes the young people were not allowed to cut and plant trees. It was not that, the young were deprived of certain rights but as per their understanding, *tain* or "old" implies qualities like wisdom/wise and worth/worthy. The philosophy is that a person of such qualities is worthy to do such things as they considered the trees, not only belonging to the Supreme Being but also respected the trees as the dwelling place of the highest being.

Festivals and ceremonies are signs of humans wanting to be in harmony with nature; rivers, trees, water. In their ceremonial song and incantations, tribals address and treat nature as they would treat their friends, parents and lovers, with much care and respect. For the Aos, festivals and ceremonies are not only for eating, drinking and merry-making but are deeply connected with the soil. These are celebrated not only to nourish and refresh themselves, but also to invoke the blessings of the Supreme Being on the soil. Most festivals are; in a nutshell, for the tribals, a celebration with the soil. The fact that the Aos are identically interrelated in all their totality of life to the whole creation is seen explicitly depicted in this song, which Aos sung during *tsiingremmong*[3] festival:

> O! In the God's dwelling place Aliyenden[4]
> Sun and moon are worshipped
> As the fig tree bear fruits
> Young men never cease dancing.

Further, they share a close communion with animals and birds. For instance, a man is told not to kill any animal when his wife is pregnant. Such restraints according to Ao elders bring well-being to the unborn child in the mother's womb. Subsequently, pregnant animals and or during breeding season are not to be killed. For killing animals during such periods would bring disaster to the household and also to the whole village community.

As they attach great importance to animals, domestic animals are also regarded as part of the family. If the chickens are hatched, the whole family will detach themselves from their normal work for three to six days to welcome the life of the new arrival in the family. During such times, everything is left to rest. It is a period of rest for the land, family and community. Free from hard work and engagement, people reflect and contemplate on their approach to agriculture, animals and the Supreme Being.

Their care and respect towards the rest of creatures is best reflected spectacularly in the day of *Ali kulemni* or the purification of the soil. The Aos observed this ritual after

---

3. Aos observed this three days festival just before the harvest season. It is a festival of worship and sacrifice offered to Lizaba, the creator God, for plenteous crops and harvest.
4. A place in an Ao village Khensa.

the new fields for cultivation are burnt. Now, during the time of the burning of the fields, animals, reptiles, and birds may have been accidentally burnt alive. The Aos consider such treatment to be inhuman and cruel. So, the eldest in the village, on the behalf of all offer a sacrifice to the deity and to the spirit of those ill treated creatures for forgiveness.

Here, I am reminded of an incident that took place years ago. As a child I often go and stay at my maternal grand-mother's house in the village. One day, as I was helping her cleaning the rice, some chicks, entered from the back door of the house and started eating the rice, which was kept lying in a bowl, on the floor. Seeing this, when I was just about to chase them away at once, I was stunned to hear my grand-mother saying to the chicks like this:

> *yangdang ja-ang-ninga yari*
> *jarai-azulo jabika aniingbiangni*

Which means stop eating-you had enough-leave the rest for your grandmother to eat. Such was the love and respect the Aos attributed even to animals.

An extract from an Ao creation poem illustrates the Ao belief that it was the birds that decide the process of days and nights:

> Oh! Originated from the six stones
> All birds are assembled
> The owl said if there is darkness
> Let there always be darkness
> For the interest of all the Impang bird said
> Let there be light and darkness alternately
> Let that process be repeated . . .

Let's take another instance that expresses a similar sentiment. Aos tell the story of how a bird helps man to find water. Originated from six stones, human beings did not know what water was. Instead they drank the juice of cane and banana trees. One day, a bird told a man called Imsenperong through a song: Imsenperong! There is water in the hole of the stone. Hearing so, he searched and found the water in a small hole in the stone.

Thus, the Supreme Being, as believed by the Aos, executes his plan and judgement through animals, natural elements and plants. For instance, it is believed by the Aos that if a cockcrows at odd times and if a hen tries to crow like a cock, a misfortune or death is likely to happen in the owner's house or in the locality.

Their myths and songs depict the whole creation as a big family with the Supreme Being as the head. In their creation myths, the picture of the whole creation discussing together animatedly, consultation and consensus, remind one of a family image.

The Aos whenever goes for hunting, they take along the dogs with them to chase the wild animals. And, when they share the prey hunted by them they keep aside an equal share for the dog, which accompanies them.

Aos tell the story of how "a woman who lived with both man and tiger." Once in an Ao village lived a woman with two husbands; a man and a tiger. The woman gave birth to both babies and cubs without the knowledge of the fathers. One day, both the tiger and the man met together at their wife's place and consequently started to fight over the wife each claiming her for himself. They started a tug of war by pulling the wife from two different directions and as a result she was torn into two parts. After the tragic incident the man just left the dead body of his wife but the tiger with utmost care gave a proper funeral to the wife by placing her in the *Leprungki*.[5] So, it is said that the Aos learn the practice of Leprungki from the tiger.

The Aos have a fantastically formulated belief in the process of "salvation," which centres on man's philosophy of life, in relation to his environment. It is basically with this holistic background that we have to understand that for the Aos, man's salvation cannot be understood apart from the well-being of the whole creation. So also the dignity of man cannot be understood apart from the dignity of the whole creation. Aos believed that to separate the human from the family of nature and the divine is to loose the meaning of life. They say:

> *nangnu sungdonglidong sararur*
> *mesenmetula hemshibla meyutsungba*
> — *kimako metetjokbeo*

Which means, if you do not care for the trees and the animals, you'll be dealt with severely on the day of Meyutsungba.[6] It is believed that such souls cannot join the ancestral family even after death but they will turn into wandering souls. They will be even denied land for

5. In the olden days, the Aos kept the dead bodies on a raised platform made of bamboo or wood called Leprungki.

6. According to the Ao tradition, Meyutsiingba is considered as the Supreme Judge on a person's death, whose judgement is purely based on the man's earthly deeds. He is also called the God of righteousness.

cultivation and would have no domestic animals to rear in the land of the dead.

The concept of salvation as understood by Aos is *Alang* or *Alangzuk*, which literally means "worth" or "redemption." So, salvation for the Aos does not relate specifically to after life. It is cosmocentric, the life affirming concern about protection, restoration, preservation, survival and the continuance of human societal and the environmental life in this world. Salvation here is not just an abstraction, it is concrete, which encompasses all aspects of life in this world. *Alang* therefore, for the Aos means the condition, context or space in which human well-being and the ultimate fulfilments are made possible. It is the condition that preserves and restores the harmonies of creation.

It is no exaggeration to say that Aos myths and legends reflect the belief about a tradition where, God, Human, Animal and Nature had a close communion. Aos believe that there is life in everything whether it be a river, mountain or a stone. They worship them by offering sacrifices since objects are perceived as the manifestation of the divine nature of God.

The tradition does not elevate man above the rest of the creation, nor do they claim for him any unique rights. Animals and trees are seen as endowed with some degree of feelings and responsibility as any human beings can be. They are depicted as threats to human beings, only when their rights are denied and not treated well.

Humans are not superior to animals. The existence of humans is not possible without animals and other creation. Without the help of animals, humans would have been in darkness without life and vitality. That is why the Aos do not think and claim that people have the absolute right and power over other objects of creation. All their myths symbolically express that humanity should not be above nature. Thus, living in harmony with the Supreme Being and with other creatures is the basis of authentic human existence.

For a tribesman, the natural phenomena are not just mere objects, but are living and dynamic. All knowledge and understanding come to them through observing the signs and listening to the voices of creation. Thus, for instance, Aos believed that the cry of the cuckoo indicates the arrival of spring, the time of sowing seeds. And, if a pet runs away and takes shelter in someone else's house, sickness or death or divorce is indicated in the owner's house.

All such beliefs are indicative of how nature occupies a central place in their life-cycle. Their life is seen synchronized fully with the rhythm of nature. Nature is the calendar, plants and birds warn about impending danger. Without nature's guidance, human life would have been floundering and directionless. Their timely warnings and signals support and sustain the life and movement of the people and help them to avoid misfortune and tragedy. To destroy and abuse the whole of creation would be like cutting the lifeline of the entire community because the very core of a tribal community and life is to be understood according to the way of nature.

As the many, the (manifoldness), have a single source or are, understood as the manifestation of a Supreme Being.

The message of their philosophy is ultimately that the reality is one. The myths and songs of their culture elevate us to a vision of the unity of all realities and lead us to a system of beliefs in a dynamic and meaningful world. Nature with all its components makes an organic, integrated and inter-related meaningful system of coherent existence. In short, it provides us with a philosophy of inseparable co-existence of all entities.

Unlike the modernists, for the Aos nature and supernatural is not something that stands radically apart from us. They use words like "mighty," "powerful," "divine". . . to describe nature and the supernatural but they are also convinced of the possibility of entering into an intimate relationship with any part of such forces, be it a tree, mountain, supernatural or a spirit.

Here the reality is seen as a web of intimate ontological relation-ships amongst men, animals, vegetables and natural forces. Beings and forces interact with each other and also influence each other. Every force, be it man, animal or rock, is entitled to a place in the scheme of things, which is given to him.

Underlying this understanding is the Aos holistic vision of life, where there is no distinction between sacred and secular, but all together constitutes wholeness of life. Such a holistic vision of life transcends the idea of dualism or duality of the Western world and establishes equality and community. According to this vision, life of alls together constitutes an organic unity. In this sense, human, nature and spirit do not stand apart from each other as opposing factors. Rather they "constitute as a basic texture of existence — what makes man truly human. Balance and harmony of man-nature-spirit are essential for man to continue to remain human."

However, the people extended the idea of respect to the natural world, not only because they conceived it as an extension of the human community. The natural world of the Aos is, of course inspirited. The legendary description of mountain, rivers and trees perceiving, deliberating and responding voluntarily as persons, however must not lead to the conclusion that they saw the natural world as same with human beings. On the contrary there is great difference between trees, rivers and us. But the difference does not amount to their devoid of each other.

The unity of nature and culture is the most profound thrust of Ao thought. Once we divorce the world of plants and animals from the world of man, difference between the two become fundamental and ineffaceable. This kind of approach, of classification and systematization, is rejected by the ancient Aos. Life is felt as an unbroken continuous whole, which does not admit of any clear-cut distinction -let us say between culture and nature. Here, the limits between the different spheres of nature and culture are not insurmountable barriers, they are fluent and fluctuating, there is no specific difference between the various realms of life. However, this also should not lead us to a conclusion that ancient Aos do not have the capacity to explain the empirical differences of things. In fact, they show an astounding knowledge of all sorts of animals, plants and rocks as I have highlighted in the discussions.

The problem of unifying two "unrelated" ideas, man and nature, into a single conceptual scheme is the problem for the radical ecologists and not for the Aos philosophy. They had a living experience of nature and a rich store of knowledge for they stood in the forest as its inhabitants and not as guests. Panger Imchen puts across this sentiment beautifully:

> There is no real distinction in the tribal cosmology that may convey the ontological separateness between the Supreme Being, spirits and humans. The indwelling spirit of God is all around them. There is no real distinction or separateness between the creator and creatures, the Being and beings and all other entities. Distinction is maintained only at the existential level.[7]

The traditional tribal society maintained an organic eco-world-view, through the practice of their *Sobaliba,* which embodies, the traditional etiquette, social manner, honesty, integrity, virtues and much more than that. It is the socio-ethical principle that enables a person to deny oneself for the sake of community. They say: *Community first then comes the individual.* Speaking on the same line Renthy Keitzar said: "we cannot explain such traditional code of morals, but these can be understood."[8] In other words, the tribal-communitarian society and an eco-friendly life cannot be sustained without the practice of moral values. And it is this principle that makes the eco-vision of the Aos a reality.

---

7. Panger Imchen, Ancient Ao-Naga Religion and Culture, New Delhi: Har-Anand Publication, 1983, p. 95.
8. Renthy Keitzar, "Tribal Theology in the Making," in *New Horizons in Ecumensians: Essays in Honour of Bishop Samuel Amrithan*, ed. K.C. Abraham, Bangalore: BTESSC & BTTBPSA, 1993, p. 48.

Though the value of non-human life is necessarily understood from the human perspective in a tribal world-view, it does not follow that human beings are the centre or measure of all value. Here, ethics is conceived primarily in the language of response and responsibility, correcting the "modern" formulation in terms of principles and rules in terms of justice. This highlights community and the common good, relates parts and whole, individuals to communities, and re-describes the community and common good to include the non-human world.

Today, what worries the modern man most is the prospect, of becoming himself a stranger to the earth, of never quite settling into it, of losing touch with the places that help constitute the identity of his community, of therefore being at home nowhere. Therefore, for the sake of our own identities we must maintain the identities of the places where we live and this entails maintaining nature. The motive for saving ecosystems may most fundamentally lie in our need to feel at home where we live — to attach ourselves to what becomes safe and secure because in one way it retains its aesthetic and cultural characteristics in the midst of change.

Without hesitation, it can be said that tribal ecology had much order, equilibrium, harmony, and it was possible to admire such nature, respect it, and form a policy of integrating society with such nature. But recent ecology has seen much disorder, disturbance, perturbation, chaos in natural systems, leaving the puzzling question whether such nature is worthy of respect and preservation. The tendency to see more chaos in ecosystems is part of a larger trend in other sciences — physics, astronomy, chemistry, climatology and mathematics — an inter-disciplinary science of chaos. Nature at the system level is often unpredictable, either in principle or too complex to be modelled. But this modern tendency to see disorder may not just be discovering objective facts about nature; it may be a projection on to nature of a "post-modernist" ideology about society, believing that societies too are fundamentally erratic.

Persons in contemporary society, however, since they have fallen into this anthropocentrism, cannot realistically undertake such a primitive return to nature. But they can perhaps reach a *self-realization,* an ecological self (in the sense advocated by Naess) that does transcend anthropocentrism.

Conclusion

At an age of mounting positivistic philosophy, environment and its preservation has been reduced only to scientific preview. The concept of preservation has been best exemplified in science — in its utilitarian, and pragmatic extension — in technology. Such reduction naturally had its adverse impact on the understanding of environment itself. "Nature" here is a means for the revelation and formulation, of the facts of science. This modern understanding viewed nature and its preservation only in a limited segment of its enterprise. This conception of nature and its preservation claimed to have immensely contributed to the growth of modem development. But as I have tried to show in the present work its vision of nature itself can also tend to be narrow.

Rather than merely taking a mechanistic view of the earth processes, where humans are continually struggling for unlimited material progress through eco-growth mediated by technological innovation, a greater appreciation of the interconnectedness of an organic, ecological view of the world is emerging. Indeed, such a world-view already exists in many artistic expression of tribals' world-view, as I have discussed at length in the fifth chapter.

This view of nature as a mechanistic, inanimate storehouse of riches and resources, to be exploited for human benefit has dominated the past several hundred years and brought with it an unprecedented abuse of the natural world. Now we are witnessing new development in science that makes such a viewpoint no longer valid. Gratefully, we are on the threshold of a new understanding of nature in which traditional religious wisdom, personal experience, and scientific insight can be mutually enriching, and produce a society in which humans are in harmony with living nature.

Today, the world is stepping into an age, signalling the most significant change in human culture where man desperately wants security based on a new form, grounded in deep reparticipation. His argument is that politics along the social set-up should give way to a new earth-directed politics and society, dedicated to preserving, enhancing and resacralizing life within the biosphere.

This vision of reality is an ecological vision, which in a sense, goes far beyond the immediate concerns of environmental preservation. But in spite of all the hype about the modem concerns for the nature and its preservation we are still left with the question — Are we satisfied with having patches of protected biodiversity in the form of nature reserves?

As such, the environmentalist and the philosopher both must re-emphasize their demands for a rethinking on the ethical dimension of life itself. Building the broken linkages between ecology, economics and ethics has become significant. It is with this spirit that the environmental preservation ethics, is taking its core from the tribal ecological wisdom.

It is accurate to say that the cultures of tribals throughout the world were permeated with nature-oriented religion that expressed the eco-centric perspectives. These cosmologies, involving a sacred sense of the earth and all its inhabitants, helped order their lives and determine their values.

For the question has the tribal eco-centered world-view anything of value to offer to modern man? The answer is yes — the tribal thought contains insight into the nature of man and environment that modern man has lost, but which is of utmost importance in dealing with environmental issues, as there is a feedback relationships between nature, culture and the individual human being. Within the scientific world-view the individual finds himself estranged from the universe, and indifferent if not hostile to nature, precisely because the scientific cosmology has made the universe a coldly inimical place for man.

As the concept of environment and culture is seen as relative, it is also important to say how one culture/civilization relate to the concept of preservation. Because, each civilization has a different attitude towards the preservation of nature. The point is, one cannot develop a sound strategy of preservation without taking into consideration one's culture. As human beings are differently moulded by the norms and ethics of their culture, preservation strategy also should start from that grassroots level, i.e., by re-evaluating or through respecting their cultural values.

Man should try to conceive of himself and his purpose not in opposition to an environment (which is beginning to fight back), but through the surrounding world, which may support him forever if he learns to base his cultures upon ideals that allow the earth to flourish.

A philosophical attitude is the primary determining factor of any human attitude — Western philosophy emphasizes the supremacy of man over the rest of the world, which only exists to serve him — or so they contend. Since, the time of Francis Bacon and Descartes, early in the seventeenth century, we have been convinced that we are the masters and possessors of nature. The prodigious progress of the sciences seems to give us the right to do what we want and so to confirm this philosophical attitude. Therefore, it is no wonder that protection of environment according to biological law, did not receive any support from Western philosophy.

Each civilization has a different attitude towards nature and wildlife. Some says that one of the best indicators of how a culture relates to the environment is its attitude towards large carnivores, who are not only an important factor in maintaining the ecological equilibrium but also a source of potential conflicts and danger to people and cattle. The relationships of the tribals of the north-eastern India with tigers provide a good picture of this idea. Hindus also believe that the tiger is the vehicle of the goddess Durga, who keeps the worlds over by fighting against demons.

In recent philosophical literature concerning the current environmental crisis the root-cause is often identified as our relentless anthropocentrism. No doubt the self-centeredness of our species is a factor for the neglect of the rest of nature. But, if we are to come to the root of the problem, we have to go deeper into the way of thinking upon which our anthropocentrism is erected. And as long as we fail to experience how intimately we belong to the earth as a part of us, we will probably not care deeply for our natural environment.

This should not lead us to conclude that all preservation ventures are destructive and exploitative. In other words, if the environment is to be salvaged, modernists have to grasp the philosophy that man is part of nature and must preserve it not for anything else but for its own sake. Such an understanding about the "environment" necessarily extends to a sweeping revision of existing ethical beliefs and "value structures." And such an attitude in every individual is determined by ones culture and tradition.

While it is common to blame modernization, commercialization and changing priorities of human beings for the environmental degradation that we see today, we must also rethink about the role played by one's world-view. And one reason for environment degradation I feel is the loss of values, and how it has led to environmental degradation. The decline in values has led to increased greed and corruption. Today devotees of Hinduism have ignored the emphasis that is given to nature. One such instance is Deepavali, the festival of lights, which now is celebrated with a lot of noise and poisonous smoke. Similarly, Holi, the festival of the colours of spring has been reduced into a dangerous chemical display. Then again devotees keep polluting the Ganga while taking a dip in the same holy river to wash away their sins. Definitely, such practices cannot have come from the foundation of Hinduism.

If we have to care for the environment, we have to go back to our roots. Nature was the center of everything. The deities and gods were symbols of natural forces. Today, the traditions and scriptures are misunderstood and misinterpreted by the modernist. Nature cannot be preserved as a museum's piece and that is exactly what is being witnessed now. It is necessary to integrate elements, which can make conservation ethic sound, and one such element is tribal eco-centric world-view.

As the modern man is blinded by his desire for advancement and development, he relates with nature only to better his life, which makes his idea to preserve the nature erroneous. The point is that modern human-centered view of nature is to account for a moral justification for the central policies of environmental preservation. The thesis of anthropocentrism is in sharp contrast with the tribal ecological ethics. Tribals believe that it is a basic ethical principle that we must respect nature as an ongoing subject of a history, a life process, a developmental system. The basis of a moral justification of tribal environmental policy is that we have ethical obligation to the natural world, just as we have ethical obligation to our fellow human beings.

Differing from the modernists, the relation seen here is neither one of domination nor of aesthetics appreciation. Tribal people are more exposed to nature than others; there is a long history of a close relation between people and nature. Nature, together with history is the basis of their sensibility. Unlike the modernist, it is a rapport with nature, which is not grasped in terms of resources for material exploitation, or an object for aesthetic contemplation. It is nature as the basis for self-respect and self-understanding. Such a way of understanding nature, and of living with it, will even transcend the ethical dimension of metaphysics.

It is no exaggeration that their myths, tales and belief system reflect about a Golden Age when God, humans, animals and nature had a close communion. And, a careful revaluation of the values embedded in them will surely enrich the "confused" modern man towards a holistic understanding about the world.

As I have shown their world-view provided them with a comprehensive vision of man and his cosmos. In that cosmos he always lived out his existence quite meaningfully. It is salutary for us to be reminded of the ineffable quality of co-creatureliness and the beauty of natural things, apprehended by these communities. They have remained closer to nature. Their dance, rituals, songs, adorns the museums, but, what is essentially human in our life of the individual and the society can be retrieved by learning from them. The point is not of going back in time. It is rather one of sensibly assessing, dynamically tracing out the thought patterns to enrich human life and nature.

Instead of perceiving nature as a subject to which man is inseparably related, modern approach reduced nature to an object from which we are totally detached and separated. Here, Nature is something "out there", apart from us and apart from God. This detachment, leads to an objective study of all, and then to manipulation and domination.

The scientific method of reductionism took the mystery out of the Western view of creation. People began to believe that there was nothing amazing about the cosmos. The physical world was viewed merely as the sum-total of many material components and energies. Within such a perspective, human's domination of creation was absolutely justified.

This is the reason why I argue that this Western science and technology, is colonial and classicist. It emerged out of a context of aggressive anthropocentrism and much a morphism. It is based on a reductionist view of life, on the theory that all matter presents a body of facts that must be objectively evaluated first, then proved and finally appropriated for human use. Thus they see that it is the Western scientific mindset that has created a wedge between man and nature.

Modern science is sometimes not aware to what extent our exercise of "reason" is eco-centric and anthropocentric. At this point, we can turn to the tribals' unique understanding of man and his idea of reason. This tribal understanding of nature should be revived to inculcate a new ethic with respect to the natural world.

The affirmation of the centrality of creation is crucial for us today because the tribal people are confronted with various survival problems. I consider this survival crisis of the tribal people as a product of the modern development paradigm in the pretext of the so-called "Reason."

Then again the whole modern concept of development is rooted in the unilinear concept of history and philosophy, it projects the modern Western industrial society as the goal to be reached and followed. In this race, the criteria for judging human society are economic and the presence of industries. This notion justifies the raping of the environment. It also makes people to think and believe that the earth-centred life and culture is "uncivilized" and "primitive."

In the conclusion, I wish to re-emphasize that modern attempts to preserve the environment, including the ecologist and environmental endeavous, are not adequate to respond to the modern environmental and the tribal peoples crisis. Modern environmental endeavous have been predominantly anthropocentric in their approaches. They are still insensitive to the environmental crisis. Therefore, they have partially contributed to the present ecological catastrophe and tribal people's suffering.

Modern man must, firstly rediscover the centrality of creation in our thoughts. Although "creation" is one of the prominent features of the entire sequel of debates, the dominant intellectual discourse has not sufficiently dealt with the issue of creation-centered world-view. This is not to argue that the dimension of creation is absent in the mainline intellectual discourse. The question here is of priority.

In short, while the doctrine of creation is a subordinate category in the mainline modern intellectual discussion, "creation" is the central key in understanding all realities in the traditional Ao world-view. That is the basic difference between the tribal and other dominant world-views.

Since the scientific exploration followed a path of division and specialization, it blinded us to see the universe as one being that acts. The tribal eco-world-view as an evaluative and relational understanding and vision of all beings in nature and the universe in their mutual interdependence has a new vision of nature preservation to offer. It is a vision of co-existential, mutually tolerant and mutually accepting and respectful way of adjustment and adaptation. It is the vision of collaboration and contribution in view of the preservation of the bio-systems, which is essential for the survival of life on this planet. This partnership vision of life implies replenishing mother earth, never with an exploitative attitude but with an attitude of preservation, promotion and stewardship and never with a dominating, violent destructive temper. In short, peaceful co-existence is at the core of their world-view.

But one should not confuse this eco-world-view of the tribals from just another fancy label for environment preservation. Rather it implies a fundamental re-orientation of perception. It is no exaggeration to say that the creation-centered vision of reality provides the modernists with a new attitude towards the earth. The earth is to be seen as the symbol of unity of all living creatures and the spirit and God. Earth is their origin, their nourishment and their identity. Such a vision of life demands a radical change in our attitude and our relationship (with the natural resources (refer chapter five). Since the whole earth is God's body and the mother, the use of the earth's resources becomes an ecological sacrament for them.

Modern environmentalists with their deep concern for environmental preservation have affirmed the importance of the relationship of man and nature but the possibility of a harmonious co-existence from this relationship is never explored. This is more so because the notion of the natural and the cultural are seen as addressing to two distinguishable orders of reality — what is humanly instituted and what is naturally ordained. This is not so in the pre-modern world-views or the traditional narratives where rocks, mountains as well as animals are positioned in the forefront along with humans. We can also see that life possess the same dignity in its highest and lowest forms. Man, animals and plants are on the same level. What is more, there is a continuous communication between them.

All such sense of inter-relatedness between the man and the natural world has formed the norm of perception and behaviour of the tribal groups. And, such a structure did not allow the separation of experience into mutually exclusive dichotomies but tends to stress modes of inter-relatedness across categories of meaning, never loosing sight of an ultimate wholeness.

To attain correlation to the whole, to all manifestation of the sacred, be they rocks, animals or people, was considered as indispensable for both personal and group well-being. For them, the ultimate purpose of life was to address an order that maintains its earth-oriented balance. It provided their people with an ethical with a strong emphasis on the right order which ruled both nature and humans and which stood for truth, right, justice and cosmic order. As such, they do not approach environmental preservation out of a sense of liability and for reasons as exhibited earlier in the discussions on most environmental ethics. The ideal of living a good life involves doing the right thing by fellow human beings, mother earth, the ancestors as well as God. Therefore, for them environment is not either for exploitation or for adulation.

According to the Ao tradition, the ground of moral evaluation is the entire environmental complex. Their concern is not — which values best enhance the interest and welfare of man, but it is about — which values enhance the overall creations and interests of the environmental complex as a whole.

Such a world-view would explain more accurately if we realize that for them the concept of the "society" is not taken of exclusively in human context. For the Aos, all life was social life and as such it was appropriate to call moral valuation a social process, as is any other human activity, since the society was explained to encompass the inseparable linkage of human behaviour to the rest of the creation.

Modern philosophical and sociological discussion seems to draw a sharp dichotomy between means and ends. I think such a dichotomy is perhaps the major cause of our sense of alienation from the rest of creation, as it presupposes that most things seem only as means aiding us in attaining our goals. Such a dichotomy between means and ends also motivated ethical theory.

Though we can make use of other beings to serve our goals, it is also necessary for us not to take only their instrumental value into account when we judge their worth. To attain such a position Western ethics is of little help. Tribesman, on the other hand had over thousands of years developed sound ethical relationships with the rest of creation based upon the insight that we all are members of a community characterized by both mutual respect and mutual use.

From an eco-centric view, all beings are valuable not simply as means but also in themselves. Here, everything from the man to the natural world is of the network of relationships that encompasses life as a whole.

> A respectful ethics is not only more in keeping with reality than a rights based one, it is also more

> demanding, for it asks us to be mindful toward all our relations.[1]

Dissatisfied with the modern Western moral principles, we can find a sounder ethical framework developed by the Aos who for thousand of years have lived in intimate proximity with all their relations. Tribesman are not bothered with developing a nature ethic but are rather concerned about a sensibility to live harmoniously which in the ultimate analysis follows from their cosmological vision that all life is sacred.

It is obvious to note how the distinction between the natural and the human has remained a pre-supposition of all Western moral, aesthetic and philosophical deliberation. Here both the ability to be moral and the ability to appreciate beauty are limited to man. Nature as the other appears beautiful only when the human self is at a safe distance from it. This kind of separating of man from other parts of creation would appear strange to the tribals. Modern ethical language is, in fact, inadequate to meet the demands tribals attributes to it.

In the traditional tribal world-view, we can ascertain attitudes, which show how unique they were from the modern man's view. Tribals' undying commitment to the interdependence of different entities precluded the man/nature dualism that basically discouraged value distinctions. In their world-view individual development and the development of the other, which includes one's environ-

---

1. Gusdizerega, "Individuality, Human and Natural Communities, and The Foundation of Ethics," in *Environmental Ethics*, 17, no. 1 (1995).

ment, are co-extensive. Such spiritual dimension which is explained simply as the ability to live virtuously in the Ao traditions, is the foundation for bringing man into closer harmony with nature while for the Western thinkers it is the way for elevating man in status over nature as both a rational and moral being.

The deep ecologist made a desperate effort to try to bridge the gap of the modern man-nature dichotomy by more alienated approaches, a conscious awakening to reintegrate what it had once disassociated from itself, namely the "other." For the tribals the relationship is one way. Such an approach makes possible communication with and for loving the other without necessarily undermining the reality of the other.

Due to the rapid spreading of modern consciousness, it has become more and more difficult for the modern man to think in terms of wholeness and as a result more difficult to understand the tribal point of view. It is true that the tribesman believes that all needs of life come from nature. But they also acknowledge nature's wrath. Their worldview is simple. If one abides by the rules then the good forces that abound in nature, come spontaneously to the rescue of good man and saves him from the evil influences of the malevolent forces.

It is paradoxical that while ecologists are inviting for a spiritual renewal that will awaken an ecological sensibility, which will make possible harmonious relationships among human and with non-human beings, the tribals that shares this harmonious relationship are being uprooted deliberately.

The present discussion however, should not lead us to assume that we should go back in time. The purpose of this exploration is to show that there are certain elements in the traditional Ao world-views, which can be integrated in our search for a new modern society. The reason is that the traditional Ao world-view is predominantly an eco-world-view, which lays great emphasis on the earth. It affirms that whole of the creation is a single family in which there is a continuous search for wholeness and meaning by each other.

Modern man must try to break the distinction between the human and the nature, by bridging the gap between the world, and ourselves emphasizing how we are the "same" instead of how we are "different". Once we realized how close we are to nature we will naturally want to preserve it. It is our alienation from earth; the divide between the human and the natural that makes us want to be master.

From the earlier discussion we have learned that it was Sobaliba (moral code) along with Yimcha (religion) that kept the link between nature and culture alike in the mind of each successive generation of Aos through legends, songs and with examples. In whatever way precisely we interpret the Ao theory of creation, the point that is significant here is that man along with fellow creatures, which includes animals, is part of nature, and God does not expect man to conquer nature but to live with them. There is a regular flow of give and take processes between man and nature.

Man, whether primitive or modern, is not at all a master of nature, he is only a child of nature. He must conform his actions to certain natural laws and order, if he is to maintain his dominance over his environment. When he tries to circumvent the law of nature, he usually destroys the natural environment that sustains him. And when his environment worsens rapidly, his civilization also declines. So man has to depend totally upon his mother earth.

The tribal eco-centered religion also demands us (the modern man) to reconsider our understanding of "salvation." Conclusion Since the self of the Supreme Being is seen in creation and humans are an integral part of it, we are able to affirm that the human attains redemption only in relation to the rest of creations. Together with God, spirit and the mother earth, we are redeemed. Such an idea of redemption further leads us to conceive salvation as a reality which can be experienced authentically "here and now." A redeemed person is the one who lives in harmony not only with God and his fellow beings, but also with the rest of creation.

Bibliography

Agera, R. Cassian, "Human Creativity, A Value? An essay in Ecological Creativity," *Religion and Society*, 42, no. 3 (September 1995) : 34-47.

Attfield, Robin, Andrew Belsey, ed., *Philosophy And Natural Environment*, Cambridge: Cambridge University Press, 1994.

_______, *The Ethics of Environmental Concern*, New York: Columbia University Press, 1983.

Barbour, Ian G., *Technology, Environment & Human Values*, New York: Praeger Publisher, 1980.

Bew, W.J., *Human Ecology*, London: Oxford University Press,1935.

Bhattacharya, N.N., *History of Indian Cosmological Ideas*, New Delhi: Munshiram Manoharlal, 1971.

Blackstone, T. William., ed., *Philosophy and Environmental Crisis*, Athens: University of Georgia Press, 1974.

Bookchin, Murray, *The Philosophy of Social Ecology: Essays on Dialectical Naturalism*, Jaipur-New Delhi: Rawat Publication, 1996.

Brennan, Andrew, *Thinking about Nature: An Investigation of Nature, Value and Ecology*, London-New York: Routledge, 1988.

Budiansky, Stephen, *Nature's Keepers: The New Science of Nature Management*, London: Free Press, 1995.

Calicott, Baird. J., "Non-Anthropocentric Value Theory and Environmental Ethics," *American Philosophical Quarterly*, 21 (1984): 299-309.

Chhatwal, Gr, D.K. Pandey, K. K. Nanda, *Encyclopedic Dictionary of Environment*, vol. IV, New Delhi: Anmol Publications, 1988.

Coates, Peter, *Nature: Western Attitudes Since Ancient Times*, Berkeley: University of California Press, 1998.

Cobb, John, W. Martin Lewis, *Green Delusions: An Environmentalist Critique of Radical Environmentalism*, Durban: Duke University Press, 1992.

Collier, John Sr., *The Indian As Ancient Man; and Ancient Man as the Primal Ecologist*, Mexico City: Homanage a Juan Comas ensu 65 Aniversario, vol. I: 15-22, 1965.

Collin, H.P., *Dictionary of Ecology and the Environment*, Middlesex: Peter Collin Publishing Ltd, 1988.

Cox, G.W., ed., *Reading in Conservation Ecology*, New York: Appleton-Century Crofts, 1969.

Cullmann, Oscar, *Salvation in History*, London: SCM Press, 1967.

Dagmann, F. Raymond, *The Conservation Alternative*, New York: John Willy & Sons, Inc. 1975.

Davis, Sandy, "Getting the Public involved: A key to Environmental Solution," *Environment and People* (September 1998) : 7-9.

Deval, Bill & George Sessions, *Deep Ecology*, Salt Lake City, Utah: Peregrine Smith Books, 1985.

Down to Earth (2000-02) — relevant issues.

Dupuis, E. Melanie & Peter Vandergeest, eds., *Creating the Countryside: The Politics of Rural and Environmental Discourse*, Philadelphia: Temple University Press, 1995.

Edwards, Paul, ed., *Encyclopedia of Philosophy*, New York: MacMillan Publishing Co. Inc., and Free Press, 1958.

Ehrenfeld, David, *The Arrogance of Humanism*, New York: Oxford University Press, 1978.

Elliot, Robert & Avran Gare, eds., *Environmental Philosophy*, Pennsylvania: State University Press, 1983.

Fanning, Odam, *Man and his Environment: Citizen Action*, London: Harper & Raw Publishers, 1975.

Ferre, Frederick, *Being and Value: Toward a Constructive Post Modern Metaphysics*, New York: State University of New York Press, 1996.

Ghosh, Ranjan, "Man and His Concepts of Nature," *Dharsana International*, 38, no. 4 (October 1998) : 17-22.

Gilkey, Longdon, *Nature, Reality and the Sacred*, Minneapolis: Fortress Press, 1993.

Good Poster, K.E. & K.M. Sayre, *Ethics and Problems of the 21st Century*, London: University Press, 1979.

Gore, Al., *Earth in the Balance: Ecology and the Human Spirit*, Boston: Houghton Mifflin, 1992.

Gransberg-Michealson, Wesley, *The Worldly Spirituality: Call to Redeem Life on Earth*, New York: Harper & Row Publisher, 1984.

______, *Ecology and Life*, Waco: Word, 1988.

Hallman, David G., *A Place in Creation: Ecological Victims in Science, Religion and Economics*, Toronto: The United Church Publishing House, 1992.

Helfrich, H.W. Jr., ed., *The Environmental Crisis*, New Haven, Conn: Yale University Press, 1970.

Hettinger, Ned, "Enhancing Natural Value?," *Human Ecology Review*, 3, no. 1 (Autumn, 1996) : 8-11.

Hossein Nar, Seyyed, *Man and Nature: The Spiritual Crisis of Modern Man*, London: Unwin Paper Packs, 1968.

Imchen, Panger, *Ancient Ao Naga Religion and Culture*, New Delhi: Har-Anand Publication, 1993.

Jha, N.V., ed., *Proceedings of the National Seminar on Environmental Awareness reflected in Sanskrit Literature*, Class E No. 11, Poona: Centre of Advanced Study in Sanskrit, University of Poona, 1991.

King, E. Grace, *Conflict and Harmony: A Source Book of Man in his Environment*, London: George Philip and Sons Limited, 1972.

Krishnamurti, J., *On Nature and the Environment*, San Francisco: Haper San Francisco, 1991.

Lamb, L. Kara, "The Problem of Defining Nature first: A Philosophical Critique of Environmental Ethics," *The Social Science Journal*, 33, no. 4 (1996) : 475-86.

Lewis, H. P., *Philosophy of Religion*, London: The English University Press, 1965.

Longchar, A. Wati, *Kechiba Libukum Anogo?*, ed. C. Wati Walling Impur: 1992.

———, *The Traditional Tribal Worldview and Modernity*, Jorhat, Assam: Published by N. Limala Longkumer Eastern Theological College, 1995.

Longchar A. Wati & Vashum Yongkahao, *The Tribal Worldview and Ecology*, Jorhat: Tribal Study Centre, 1998.

Mahanti, Neeti, *Tribal Issues: A Non-Conventional Approach*, New Delhi: Inter-India Publication, 1994.

Merchant, Carolyn, ed., *Ecology: Key Concepts in Critical Theory*, Jaipur: Rawat Publications, 1960.

Milton, Kay, *Environmentalism and Cultural Theory: Exploring the role of Anthropology in Environmental Discourse*, London: Routledge, 1996.

Miri, Sujata, *Ethics and Environment: Theory and the Adi and Khasi Practice*, Delhi-Guwahati: Spectrum Publication, 2001.

Mott, Mann, J., *God in Creation: An Ecological Doctrine of Creation*, London: SCM Press, 1982.

Naess, Arne, *Ecology, Community and Lifestyle*, Cambridge: Cambridge University Press, 1989.

Passmore, John, *Man's Responsibility for Nature*, London: Routledge, 1988.

Patil, M. Subhash, "Environmental Legislation: An Overview," *Environment and People*, (August 1998) : 13-31.

Peterson, Anna, "Environmental Ethics and the Social Construction of Nature," *Environmental Ethics*, 21 (Winter 1999) : 339-57.

Rachesl, James & Frank A. Tillman, *A Philosophical Issues: A Contemporary Introduction*, New York: Harper & Row Publication, 1972.

Ramachandra, *Social Ecology*, New Delhi: Oxford University Press, Bombay, 1994.

Rasmussen, L. Larry, *Earth Community: Earth Ethics*, Geneva: WCC Publications, 1977.

Reich, A. Charles, *The Greeening of America*, New York: Bantam, 1970.

Rolston, Holmes, *Environmental Ethics: Duties to and Values to Natural World*, Philadelphia: Temple University, 1988.

Saraswati, Baidyanath, ed., *The Cultural Dimension of Ecology*, New Delhi: D.K. Printworld (P) Ltd., 1998.

Schaeffer, Francis A, *Pollution and the Death of Man: The Christian View of Ecology*, Wheaton: Tyndale House, 1970.

Sen, Getti, ed., *Indigenous Vision: People of India attitude to the Environment*, New York: Orbis Books, 1977.

Shepherd, Paul & Andrew Bebey, ed., *The Subversive Science: Essays towards Ecology of Man*, Boston: Houghton Mifflin Company, 1969.

Sinclair, John (Editor-in-chief), *Collins Cobuild English Language Dictionary*, Birmingham: Collins Publishers, 1987.

Skolimowski, Henryk, *Eco-Philosophy: Designing New Tactics for Living*, Boston, London: Marion Boyars, 1981.

Sylvan, Richard and David, *The Greening of Ethics*, Cambridge, UK: Whitehorse Press, 1994.

Taylor, Paul, *Respect for Nature: A Theory of Environmental Ethics*, Princeton, N.J: Princeton University Press, 1986.

Thomas, M.M, *Salvation and Humanization*, Bangalore: CISRS, 1961.

Thompson, Janna, "Environment as Cultural Heritage," *Environmental Ethics*, 22 (Fall 2000) : 241-58.

Ursul, A.D, *Philosophy and the Ecological Problem of Civilization*, Institute of Philosophy, USSR Academy of Sciences, 1983.

Viegas, Phillips & Geeta Menon, *The Impact of Environmental Degradation on People*, New Delhi: Indian Social Institute, 1988.

Walling, C. Walu, *Sacrifice and Salvation in Ao Naga Tradition: A Theological Perspective*, Impur, Nagaland: Published by C. Walu Walling, 1997.

White, Lynn, Jr., "The Historical Roots of our Ecological Crisis," *Ecology and Life*, Wesley Granberg — Michaelson. Waco: Word, 1988.

Zimmerman, Michael, *Contesting Earth's Future: Radical Ecology and Post Modernity*, Berkeley: University of California Press, 1994.

Index